EU Public Procurement Law

David Medhurst
Barrister, Temple

Blackwell
Science

© David Medhurst 1997
Blackwell Science Ltd
Editorial Offices:
Osney Mead, Oxford OX2 0EL
25 John Street, London WC1N 2BL
23 Ainslie Place, Edinburgh EH3 6AJ
350 Main Street, Malden
  MA 02148 5018, USA
54 University Street, Carlton
  Victoria 3053, Australia

Other Editorial Offices:
Blackwell Wissenschafts-Verlag GmbH
  Kurfürstendamm 57
  10707 Berlin, Germany

Zehetnergasse 6
A-1140 Wien
Austria

First published 1997

Set in 11/13 pt Palatino
By DP Photosetting, Aylesbury, Bucks
Printed and bound in Great Britain by
Hartnolls Ltd, Bodmin, Cornwall

The Blackwell Science logo is a trade mark
of Blackwell Science Ltd, registered at the
United Kingdom Trade Marks Registry

DISTRIBUTORS

Marston Book Services Ltd
PO Box 269
Abingdon
Oxon OX14 4YN
(*Orders:* Tel: 01235 465500
           Fax: 01235 465555)

USA
  Blackwell Science, Inc.
  Commerce Place
  350 Main Street
  Malden, MA 02148 5018
  (*Orders:* Tel: 800 759 6102
             617 388 8250
             Fax: 617 388 8255)

Canada
  Copp Clark Professional
  200 Adelaide St, West, 3rd Floor
  Toronto, Ontario M5H 1W7
  (*Orders:* Tel: 416 597-1616
             800 815-9417
             Fax: 416 597-1617)

Australia
  Blackwell Science Pty Ltd
  54 University Street
  Carlton, Victoria 3053
  (*Orders:* Tel: 3 9347 0300
             Fax: 3 9347 5001)

A catalogue record for this title
is available from the British Library

ISBN 0-632-03813-6

Library of Congress
Cataloging-in-Publication Data

Medhurst, David.
    EU public procurement law/
  David Medhurst.
      p. cm.
    Includes bibliographical references
  and index.
    ISBN 0-632-03813-6 (hc)
    1. Government purchasing—Law and
  legislation—European Union countries.
  2. Letting of contracts—European Union
  countries.
  I. Title
  KJE5632.M43 1997
  841.7'53—dc21
                            97-26
                            CIP

Contents

Preface

I have written this book in order to supply a straightforward guide for lawyers and procurement managers who have to approach, for the first time, the new, burgeoning and absurdly complicated European Union law relating to public and utilities procurement. For the benefit of lawyers I have endeavoured to give some idea of how professional buyers approach their work, because that is the key to understanding the European directives in this area. Although the book deals with some very complex law I have tried to make the language as plain as possible, in the hope that it will prove of value to buyers, suppliers, managers and others who are affected by the new regime, as well as to lawyers in private practice, local and central government, and the utilities. I have included a chapter on compulsory competitive tendering in order to show how this relates to the European law.

The Procurement Directives have existed for a number of years, but there is still widespread ignorance about their effects. The possibility of suing a government department, a public utility or a local authority for damages, or of obtaining an injunction, if any of these bodies fails to follow the purchasing procedures set out in the directives, is not always appreciated, although there is now a growing body of precedent.

There are now many companies dealing with water, energy and public transport that have to comply with the requirements of the directives.

In 1997 the Commission will make some amendments to the Directives in order to align them with the Government Purchasing Agreement. Fortunately, as this book was being prepared for the press the Commission published its proposal for the amendment of the Utilities Directive. Therefore, in an appendix (see page 195), I have been able to note the main effects of this proposal. I have also been able to include a paragraph on the recent Commission green paper on procurement; this does not presage any major changes to the structure of the law.

I have contrived to reduce the complexity of the Directives to a short compass, not as a substitute for the text of the Directives, and their implementing regulations, but to enable the reader to know where to look.

David Medhurst
February 1997

Acknowledgement

I am indebted to Jeremy Chipperfield for his help in research and the preparation of the tables and index for this book.

David Medhurst

Chapter 1

Introduction

The State undertakes public works, builds roads, cares for our health, educates us, keeps public order, and defends us from our enemies. In order to do this, the State must buy supplies and services, and place contracts for its works. The State regulates our water, energy, transport, and telecommunications industries, and therefore it can influence the way in which these utilities choose their suppliers and contractors. The money for this public procurement, that is to say purchases by or under the control of the State, accounts for some 15% of gross domestic product in the Member States of the European Union. The money comes from xenophobic taxpayers, and is spent by civil servants with no commercial sense, on behalf of patriotic politicians. Naturally, the State prefers to place its contracts with its own nationals, and to put foreigners at a disadvantage that acts as a barrier to trade. But the European Union is opposed to any such obstacles between Member States, and this is why article 7A of the Treaty on Establishing the European Community creates an internal market comprising an area without internal frontiers, in which the free movement of goods, persons, services and capital is ensured in accordance with the provisions of the Treaty.

The main provisions of the Treaty, on free movement, are as follows. Article 30 states that quantitative restrictions on imports and all measures having equivalent effect are prohibited between Member States. Article 52 abolishes restrictions on the freedom of establishment, and article 59 abolishes restrictions on freedom to provide services. Article 67 requires Member States to abolish restrictions on movement of capital. Article 85 prohibits agreements, decisions by associations of undertakings, and concerted practices that may affect trade between Member States. And article 92 declares that any State aid that threatens to distort competition is incompatible with the common market.

Unfortunately the provisions of the Treaty alone have not effectively dissuaded Member States from practising discrimination in their procurement decisions. The Council of the European Community has therefore devised a set of laws calculated to prune our xenophobic urges and ensure that public contracts are awarded openly and fairly. These laws are known collectively as the *Purchasing Directives*. They compel entities controlled or influenced by the State, including central government, local government, and the utilities, to advertise their larger contracts in the *Official Journal of the European Communities*, and to follow strict procedures in choosing their works contractors, suppliers, and service providers. The procedures stipulate the kinds of specifications that can be used, set time limits for the delivery of bids, and restrict the criteria for the award of contracts.

The first measure to be adopted by the Council in this field was the Public Works Directive, Council Directive 71/305 (OJ L185 15.8.71 p5). This was followed by the Public Supplies Directive, Council Directive 77/62 (OJ L13 15.1.77 p1). Both of these directives have now been repealed and replaced. The early regime was not successful, because the original directives contained no arrangements for their enforcement. That defect has been remedied, and it is now possible for an aggrieved supplier, works contractor or service provider to bring an action in the High Court to suspend the purchasing procedure, for damages or an injunction, if the correct procedure has not been followed.

As originally promulgated, the Purchasing Directives did not affect the procurement practices of the utilities, the *excluded sectors* as they were called: that is, entities that provide water, energy, transport and telecommunications. The reason for the exclusion of the utilities was that it was felt that it would not be possible to formulate a regime extending across both the public and private sectors. That difficulty has now been overcome by creating a directive, the Utilities Directive, that applies only to that sector. It is less prescriptive than the directives that apply in the public sector.

The public procurement regime

In order to understand the public procurement regime the reader must refer to six main directives. Four of these directives set out the detailed procedures that must be followed when entities award public contracts:

- Council Directive 93/37/EEC of 14 June 1993 concerning the coordination of procedures for the award of public works contracts (OJ L199 9.8.93 p54);

- Council Directive 93/36/EEC co-ordinating procedures for the award of public supply contracts (OJ L199 9.8.93 p1);

- Council Directive 92/50 relating to the coordination of procedures for the award of public service contracts (OJ L209 24.7.92 p1);

- Council Directive 93/38/EEC of 14 June 1993 coordinating the procurement procedures of entities operating in the water, energy, transport and telecommunications sectors (OJ L199 9.8.93 p84) .

The above directives are known respectively as the Works, Supplies, Services, and Utilities Directives. They are all, save for the Services Directive, consolidating directives, with a long history of amendments. The common features of these directives are discussed in Chapter 2, and each directive in turn is then considered in Chapters 5–8. The Directives set out procedures that must be followed by purchasing entities in order to ensure that contracts are awarded openly. The Directives affect contracts worth more than certain threshold values, and these values are tabulated in Chapter 2. In order to accommodate changes made to the international arrangements for trade and embodied in the GATT (now WTO) Government Purchasing Agreement (the GPA), the Directives will be amended. The amendment had not been passed at the time of writing, but Commission proposals have been formulated, and are published in the *Official Journal* (OJ C138 3.6.95 p1 and OJ C138 3.6.95 p44).

There are two directives, the Compliance Directive and the Utilities Remedies Directive, that require Member States to make adequate arrangements for aggrieved suppliers, service providers and contractors to seek redress if they are unfairly treated, or if the procedures set out in the Purchasing Directives are not followed. The full titles of these two directives are as follows:

- Council Directive 89/665 of 21 December 1989 on co-ordination of the laws, regulations and administrative provisions relating to the application of review procedures to the award of public supply and public works contracts (OJ L395 30.12.89 p33);

- Council Directive 92/13/EEC of 25 February 1992 co-ordinating the laws, regulations and administrative provisions relating to the application of Community rules on the procurement procedures of entities operating in the water, energy, transport and telecommunications sectors (OJ L 76 23.3.92 p14).

When reference is made in this book to the 'Directives' it may be taken to mean the six directives listed above and their amendments, or such of those directives as the context makes clear. Reference will also be made to the Supplies Directive, the Works Directive, the Services Directive, the Utilities Directive, the Compliance Directive, and the Utilities Remedies Directive. The meaning of these terms is explained above; it is usually confusing to refer to the number of a Directive, because at each consolidation the number will change.

Implementation

As far as the United Kingdom is concerned the Directives are implemented by a series of regulations made by the Treasury in the exercise of its powers under section 2(2) of the European Communities Act 1972; in this book we shall refer to the United Kingdom implementing regulations simply as the 'Regulations'. There is no danger of confusion in using the word 'regulations' because no European Regulations have been made in this area. The relevant regulations at the time of writing were as follows:

- The Public Supply Contracts Regulations (SI 1995 No 201);
- The Public Services Contracts Regulations (SI 1993 No 3228)
- The Public Works Contracts Regulations (SI 1991 No 2680);
- The Utilities Supply and Works Contracts Regulations (SI 1992 No 3279).

In practice

What this legislation means in practice is that purchasers in the buying departments of government, government-controlled bodies, local authorities, and the utilities have to dance a complicated bureaucratic jig before they can buy anything. The main steps are as follows:

- *Step 1*
  A prior indicative notice must be published in the *Official Journal* giving the supplies and services purchasing requirement for the financial year. In the case of a public sector works contract, a prior information notice is published as soon as possible after the decision approving the planning of the work.

- *Step 2*
  As soon as it is clear that a particular purchase is needed, the contracting entity must decide which of three procedures to use: the *open procedure*, where anyone can bid; the *restricted procedure*, where a shortlist may bid; and the *negotiated procedure*, where the entity simply negotiates with the suppliers of its choice. In the public sector the negotiated procedure may be used only in exceptional cases, such as where there is no response to an open procedure, cases of extreme urgency, or where articles are manufactured purely for research purposes. In the private (utilities) sector there is a free choice, provided that a call for competition has been made.

- *Step 3*
  The entity must advertise its requirement by means of a notice placed in the *Official Journal*, unless it is using the negotiated procedure, in which case a notice is sometimes not necessary. The notice must state the criteria for the award,

and this can be on the basis of either the lowest price or that most economically advantageous to the entity. Technical specifications must be defined by reference to national standards implementing European standards, or common standards drawn up with a view to uniform application in all the Member States.

- *Step 4*
  The entity must wait a specified number of days for the receipt of tenders. Under the open procedure in the Supplies Directive, for example, the entity must fix as the last date for the receipt of tenders a period of not less than 52 days from the date of dispatch of the notice.

- *Step 5*
  The entity must award the contract using the stated award criteria.

- *Step 6*
  A notice must be published in the *Official Journal* stating who was awarded the contract.

The nature of the system is described in Chapter 2, where we deal with the features common to all the Directives. More details are given in Chapters 5–8, in which we consider each directive in turn. Each of the directives contains differences of detail brought about by the nature of the contracts involved, and the whims of the Commission. The Utilities Directive has the least in common with the other directives; this is because it is designed to accord as far as possible with commercial practices in the private sector.

The complexity of the Purchasing Directives means that a purchasing department must adopt a high degree of pre-planning. First the buyer must consider whether a procurement is contemplated. If it is, then he must consider which directive (and which implementing regulation) should apply. Next he must consider some general exclusions, because some contracts (for example certain defence contracts, and secret security contracts) are excluded from the Directives. Then he must consider what award procedure is to be used. He must then consider whether a call for competition is required, and if so what will be needed to comply with that requirement.

Jargon

Public procurement has created its own jargon, and a facility with this language, which has all the beauty of Klingon, will give the desired impression of expertise. The following paragraph is intended to give not legal definitions, but the common usage.

An *entity* means a person, authority, company, organisation or whatever that does purchasing and falls within the scope of the Directives; it does not have to take on any particular legal form. A *utility* means an entity operating in the water, energy, transport and telecommunications sector within the scope of the Utilities Directive. The Directives do not apply to a contract unless its value exceeds a certain amount, known as a *threshold*. *Aggregation* means that in order to determine the threshold value of a contract the buyer must take account of, for example, all the contracts for supplying goods of a particular kind for the year. A *PIN* means a prior indicative notice or prior information notice. It is but one of the notices that an entity has to publish in the *Official Journal of the European Communities*, and it is designed to indicate to potential bidders the procurement requirement of the entity in the following financial year. Other notices are the *contract notice*, by which the entity makes known that it intends to award a particular contract and invites bids, and the *award notice*, by which it makes known the name of the person to whom it has awarded the contract. The notices appear in the *Official Journal*, and in a database known as *TED* (Tenders Electronic Daily). *Award criteria* means the criteria that can be used, either price or economic advantage, in awarding a contract.

Various *nomenclatures* are in use for the purpose of describing items in contract notices. The *Common Procurement Vocabulary (CPV)* is the nomenclature that the Commission now recommends for use in drafting contract notices. It consists of a series of nine-digit numbers, each designating one of some 6000 terms commonly used in procurement, and it is hoped that by use of this code computers will be able to scan and translate the contract notices. For example, the code for unfrozen crustaceans is 05002100-0. The CPV is based upon the *Classification of Products by Activity (CPA)*, which is a list of products by activity primarily designed for statistical purposes, which is turn is based on the *Common Product Classification of the United Nations (CPC)*. The

Statistical classification of economic activities in the European Community (NACE) is also used.

Professional buyers have terms of art to describe the processes used in their profession. *Partnership sourcing* is a term used by buyers when they have a cosy relationship with the supplier and are content to put up with his failings in order to develop a long-term relationship, like a wife with an honest husband. *Vendor appraisal* means the process by which the supplier is appraised to assess his capability to perform the contract. *Vendor rating* is a term used for the systematic assessment of how he has performed. For each supplier a record is kept under a number of headings, such as quality, delivery, and after-sales service, and according to his rating one supplier can be evaluated against another. A *framework agreement* means an arrangement (not necessarily a contract) whereby a supplier or service provider undertakes to provide goods or services, up to a certain amount, over a given period of time, and at a certain price.

Various organisations are financed by the Commission to develop standards for use in the Community. *CEN* is the European Committee for Standardisation. *CENELEC* is the European Committee for Electrotechnical Standardisation. *EN* means a European Standard. *ETSI* means the European Telecommunications Standards Institute, and *ETS* is a European telecommunications standard.

PFI means the *Private Finance Initiative,* a scheme created by the UK government whereby private finance is used in partnership with public finance for such projects as the Channel Tunnel Rail Link. Companies that become involved with PFI may find that they are subjected to the Public Procurement Directives. *CCT* means *compulsory competitive tendering,* a system that obliges local government authorities in the UK to put out work to open tender before offering it to *direct labour organisations (DLOs)* or *direct service organisations (DSOs). VFM* means value for money, which is what government wants but curiously cannot get.

Public procurement in context

The Procurement Directives are part of a new area of law, that of regulated procurement. They are set in a national, European, and world framework of laws. In order to set the Procurement Directives in context the reader must be aware of the common law background, the UK legislation on compulsory competitive tendering (CCT), the relevant provisions of the Treaty Establishing the European Community, and the terms of the WTO Agreement on Government Purchasing (GPA). The GPA is an international agreement, which emerged from the Uruguay Round of trade negotiation between the GATT (General Agreement on Tariffs and Trade) signatories, and was made on 15 April 1994. These negotiations have resulted in a new arrangement of world trade under the World Trade Organisation (WTO), which has replaced GATT.

Common law

Even when the Purchasing Directives do not apply, a purchasing authority may be bound to consider in a fair manner all the tenders submitted to it. Thus in *Blackpool and Fylde Aero Club Ltd v. Blackpool Borough Council* [1990] 1 WLR 1195, [1990] 3 All ER 25 a dispute arose about an invitation to tender for the right to operate pleasure flights from Blackpool Airport (see Chapter 9, where the facts are considered in more detail). The invitation said that the council did not bind itself to accept any tender. Two tenders were received: the first was opened, but the council did not realise that the second was in its postbox. Thinking that there was only one tender, it awarded the contract to the first candidate. The second tenderer brought an action for breach of contract. The case turned on whether the council was bound to consider any offer that was made in response to its invitation to tender. In general, the law is that an invitation to tender does not bind the invitor to consider any offer. But the Court of Appeal said that in this case a contract was to be implied because the tenders were solicited from selected parties, all of them known to the council, and the invitation prescribed a clear, orderly and familiar procedure. The tenderer was protected at least to the extent that if he submitted a tender he was entitled to have it considered, or at least considered if others were. The case is therefore authority for the proposition that at common law there are circumstances in which, by putting out a contract to tender, an authority will bind itself to consider all the bids, and it is submitted that if this is so the authority must also be bound to consider each bid by the same criteria and fairly one against another.

Compulsory competitive tendering

The United Kingdom has made national laws on compulsory competitive tendering (CCT). CCT is concerned to deny the staff of local authorities the luxury of doing work without competing for it. The law is contained in the Local Government Planning and Land Act 1980, the Local Government Act 1988, and the Local Government Act 1992. The first of these three Acts prevents local authorities from entering into building contracts through their direct labour organisations unless the contract is put out to tender. The Local Government Act 1988 widened the scope of CCT to a list of defined authorities (mainly local authorities, but also including authorities responsible for urban development, new towns, police and metropolitan transport) and a list of defined activities such as the collection of refuse and the cleaning of buildings. The effect of the 1988 Act is that there is a broad range of activities that an authority cannot carry out unless it first puts the work out to tender. Both the 1980 and the 1988 Act have been amended by the Local Government Act 1992, and the effect of this amendment has been to extend CCT to white collar activities, such as legal services. The three Acts are supplemented by a number of statutory instruments, and the system is explained in more detail in Chapter 4. The important thing to know about CCT is that it is designed to introduce market forces into the services offered by local authorities, and consequently differs in its object from the Purchasing Directives. It is concerned only with preventing authorities from doing work that, from an economic point of view, they ought not to do; for this reason it does not cover the purchasing of supplies. The two regimes overlap but rarely conflict. When there is a conflict between the CCT rules and the Directives it is the European Law that prevails.

The Government Purchasing Agreement

At an international level, procurement is regulated by the new Agreement on Government Purchasing (GPA). This emerged from the Uruguay Round of trade negotiation between the GATT signatories and was made on 15 April 1994. At the time of writing the signatories to this agreement were: the EU, Canada, Israel, Japan, the Republic of Korea, Norway, Switzerland, and the USA. By Decision 94/800/EC (OJ L336 23.12.94 p1) the Council approved the agreement. Unlike its predecessor, which applied only to central government purchasing of supplies, the new agreement extends to purchases of supplies, works and services by public bodies in both central and local government, as well as purchases by public bodies in the port, airport, water, urban transport and electricity sectors. The value of procurement under the new GPA will be in the order of 350 billion ECU each year. In order to accommodate the difficulties that buyers have in following two legal regimes, the Directives are proposed to be amended so as to align them with the GPA. The proposal has been published in the *Official Journal* (OJ 1995 C138/1). At the time of writing this proposal had not been implemented, nor had there been any formal notification of the thresholds that are applied under the Directives following the GPA. An informal notice has been circulated, and it is upon this notice that the information relating to the level of thresholds is based in this book. The GPA threshold applies, save where the EU threshold is lower.

The new thresholds are expressed in Special Drawing Rights (SDRs), whereas the old thresholds were expressed in ECU. For central government supplies and service contracts, by entities listed in Schedule 1 of the Public Supply Contracts Regulations (SI 1995/201), other than for research and development (R&D does not come within the GPA), the threshold is 130,000 SDR (the sterling equivalent is £108,667); for the purchase of supplies and services by other public authorities the GPA threshold is 200,000 SDR, but because this is above the level set by the Directives, namely 200,000 ECU (sterling equivalent £158,018), the latter prevails. The only practical relevance of the higher GPA threshold in this context is that a non-EU GPA signatory will have rights of remedy under the GPA agreement only if the value of the contract exceeds the GPA threshold. For utilities the threshold for supplies and services after the GPA is 400,000 ECU (£316,036) for energy water and transport sectors, and 600,000 ECU (£475,055) for the telecommunications sector; the EC threshold applies because the WTO Government Procurement Agreement threshold is marginally lower at 400,000 SDR. For construction contracts after the GPA the threshold is 5,000,000 ECU (£3,950,456); the GPA threshold is a little lower at 5,000,000 SDR. It is the sterling equivalent of these thresholds, as set by the Commission, that the buyer has to know. The sterling figures above are those that apply from January 1996. The various thresholds are tabulated in Chapter 2.

In order to ensure that suppliers in the European Union will benefit from treatment that is as favourable as that reserved for suppliers from third countries, it is proposed to align the provisions of the Directives with those of the Agreement. The proposal formulated by the Commission for a European Parliament and Council directive amending all the Purchasing Directives relates not only to the thresholds but to other matters. The Commission wants to simplify the Directives: of course that will not be the effect – they will simply be made more complicated. The GPA allows for derogations and exceptions not to be found in the Directives, but the Commission has proposed to keep its stricter regime because it does not wish to upset the *acquis communautaire*.

The Treaty and its jurisprudence

In order to appreciate the Purchasing Directives in their proper context, the reader must understand those elements of the European Community Treaty that relate to competition and free movement. A contract that is not affected by the directives may be affected by directly applicable articles in the Treaty, and failure to comply with a Directive will also involve a failure to obey the Treaty. The Directives are no more than a means of ensuring that the principle of equal treatment and the four freedoms (free movement of goods, services, workers and capital) are respected when large contracts are made by government, local authorities and utilities. This is done by making the transactions of such entities transparent: that is, by making those responsible for procurement accountable for their actions.

Article 30

Articles 30 and 34 of the Community Treaty forbid quantitative restrictions on imports or exports (note that this applies in both ways) and all measures having equivalent effect, between Member States. There is a derogation, to allow for considerations of health and public policy, in article 36. The articles read as follows:

- *Article 30*
  Quantitative restrictions on imports and all measures having equivalent effect shall ... be prohibited between Member States.

- *Article 34*
  Quantitative restrictions on exports, and all measures having equivalent effect, shall be prohibited between Member States.

- *Article 36*
  The provisions of article 30 to 34 shall not preclude prohibitions or restrictions on imports, exports or goods in transit justified on grounds of public morality, public policy or public security; the protection of health and life of humans, animals or plants; the protection of national treasures possessing artistic, historic or archaeological value; or the protection of industrial and commercial property. Such prohibitions or restrictions shall not, however, constitute a means of arbitrary discrimination or a disguised restriction on trade between Member States.

Article 30 was important in the decision of the European Court in the *Dundalk* case, *Commission v. Ireland* (45/87) [1988] ECR 4929, [1989] 1 CMLR 225, a judgment that shows that, irrespective of the minutiae of the Purchasing Directives, there is a requirement to avoid discriminatory practices in tendering procedures. Dundalk District Council published a notice in the *Official Journal of the European Communities* inviting tenders for a contract to lay pipes for its water system. Nowadays such a notice would be obligatory, but at that time the Directives did not apply to a contract placed by a water supply utility. Nevertheless, the Dundalk Council published a notice because it hoped to obtain Community finance for its project. The specification said that the supplier had to be certified as manufacturing pipes to the Irish standard, but there was only one manufacturer (Irish, of course) who was so certified. An engineering contractor submitted three tenders. One was based upon the use of asbestos cement pipes from the Irish manufacturer; the pipes were exactly as specified. The second tender was based on iron pipes from a UK company. The third was based on pipes manufactured by a Spanish company, which complied with BS and ISO standards.

The third tender offered the lowest price, and the pipes were of comparable quality with, if not better than, the pipes made to the Irish standard, but nevertheless that bid was rejected. The Spanish manufacturer complained to the Commission, who subsequently brought an action against the Irish government. The latter argued that because the Directives did not apply to the contract there was no breach of Community law. But the European Court found that even if the Directives did not apply there was still a breach of article 30 of the Treaty, because the specification had an effect equivalent to a restriction on imports. The Irish government also failed, in a defence based on article 36, to establish that the specification was necessary for the protection of public health, because a less restrictive specification would have sufficed for that purpose.

Dassonville and the rule of reason

Two well-known judgments of the European Court, the *Dassonville* and *Branntwein* cases, define respectively the scope and the necessary limitations of article 30. The definition of the meaning of 'equivalent effect' in article 30 is commonly known as the *Rule in Dassonville*, and this states that all trading rules enacted by Member States that are capable of hindering directly or indirectly, actually or potentially, intra-Community trade are to be considered as measures having effect equivalent to quantitative restrictions: see *Procureur du Roi* v. *Dassonville* (8/74) [1974] ECR 837, [1974] 2 CMLR 436. This is subject, however, to a rule of reason as set out in *Rewe-Zentral AG* v. *Bundesmono-*

polverwaltung für Branntwein (120/78) [1979] ECR 649, [1979] 3 CMLR 494, otherwise known as the *Cassis de Dijon* case. The problem in the latter case was that French liqueurs could not be imported into Germany because of German requirements as to their alcohol content. The Court of Justice held that the fixing of minimum alcohol content for alcoholic beverages fell within article 30, but observed that it would be possible to protect the consumer by requiring an indication of origin, and of the alcohol content, in the packaging of products; but that requirement would have to be subject to the principle of proportionality. *Cassis de Dijon* thus deals with the problems that arise when obstacles to movement within the Community result from disparities between national laws relating to marketing of products. In the absence of common rules, on the marketing of alcohol for example, such anomalies are bound to arise, and will be defended by the Member State concerned on grounds such as protection of the consumer. The rule that the Court has developed to deal with such problems is known as the *Rule of Reason*. It is a justification for conduct which might fall within article 36, but it does not derive from article 36. In the *Cassis de Dijon* case the Court expressed the rule as follows:

> Obstacles to movement within the Community resulting from disparities between the national laws relating to the marketing of the products in question must be accepted in so far as those provisions may be recognised as being necessary in order to satisfy mandatory requirements relating in particular to the effectiveness of fiscal supervision, the protection of public health, the fairness of commercial transactions and the defence of the consumer.

The rule is of general application, and therefore should provide a defence in some instances to apparent breaches of the Directives: for example, a policy by which a government department gave preference to goods manufactured in factories set up for the benefit of the disabled would not necessarily contravene either article 30 of the Treaty or the Directives.

State aid

The rule in *Dassonville* was relied on in Case C-21/88 *Du Pont de*

Nemours v. *Carrara Health Authority* [1990] ECR 889, [1982] 3 CMLR 382. The facts of this case were concerned with Italian rules under which a percentage of public supply contracts were reserved to undertakings located in the regions of the Mezzogiorno in Southern Italy. The European Court ruled that article 30 must be interpreted as precluding national rules that reserve to undertakings established in particular regions of a national territory a proportion of public supply contracts. The case is also important for its clarification of the relationship between the Treaty provisions on State aid and those concerning free movement. The question posed was whether the Italian rules might be regarded as aid within article 92 of the Treaty, and thus exempt from the prohibition set out in article 30. On this the Court held that article 92 may not be used to frustrate the rules on the free movement of goods, because articles 30 and 92 have a common purpose, namely the free movement of goods between Member States under normal conditions of competition.

Free movement of persons, services and capital

Free movement of persons, services and capital and the right of establishment are assured by the EC Treaty. Article 48 secures the right to freedom of movement for workers within the European Union. Article 52 abolishes restrictions on the freedom of establishment of nationals of a Member State in the territory of another Member State. Freedom of establishment includes the right to take up and pursue activities as a self-employed person, and to set up and manage undertakings on a basis of equality with nationals of the host State. Article 59 abolishes restrictions on freedom to provide services within the European Union. Article 58 states that, as far as freedom of movement and establishment are concerned, companies are to be treated in the same way as natural persons. Article 73(b), within a framework set out in the Treaty, abolishes all restrictions on the movement of capital between Member States. All of these freedoms are necessary to enable businesses to provide goods and services in response to requests to tender under the Procurement Directives.

Thus, in Case 76/81 *Transporoute et Travaux SA* v. *Minister of Public Works* [1982] ECR 417, [1982] 3 CMLR 382 the Luxembourg Administration des Ponts et Chaussées issued a notice inviting tenders for work on the motorway at Arlon. A Belgian company, Transporoute, submitted the lowest tender, but this was rejected in favour of a Luxembourg contractor. The excuse was that Transporoute was not in possession of an establishment permit issued by the Luxembourg government, and also it was said that the tender could not truthfully be said to be economically the most advantageous because it was abnormally low having regard to the extent of the work. The European Court said that here there was a breach of specific provisions of Council Directive 71/305/EEC (the Works Directive as it then was), namely articles 23 to 26 precluding a Member State from requiring a tenderer to furnish proof of his standing by means other than those set out in the Directive, and, as the Court interpreted it, article 29 required a purchasing authority to allow a contractor to give an explanation for its abnormally low offer before awarding the contract elsewhere. But the Court also justified its decision by direct reference to the Treaty, because its interpretation of the Directive was, said the Court, in conformity with the Treaty provisions concerning the provision of services in one Member State by a contractor established in another, and to read it in any other way would deprive article 59 of the Treaty of all effectiveness, the purpose of that article being precisely to abolish restrictions on the freedom to provide services by persons who are not established in the State in which the services are to be provided.

In Case 3/88 *Commission* v. *Italy* [1989] ECR 4035, [1991] 2 CMLR 115 the Court said that articles 52 and 59 of the Treaty embody specific instances of the general principle of equal treatment, which prohibits not only overt discrimination by reason of nationality, but also all covert forms of discrimination. Under Italian laws on the introduction of computers in the public administration only companies in which either the whole, or a majority, of the shares were held directly or indirectly by the State could conclude agreements with the Government. The Court held those provisions to be incompatible with articles 52 and 59.

That case was followed by the *Lottmatica* case, Case C-272/91 *Commission* v. *Italy* [1994] ECR I-1409, [1995] 2 CMLR 673. In Italy only the State may conduct lotteries. In November 1990 the Italian Finance Ministry published a contract notice for the concession for the computerisation of the Italian Lotto. The right to tender was restricted to bodies the majority of whose capital was held by the public sector. The Commission brought proceedings in which it claimed that by so doing Italy had failed to comply with its obligations under articles 30, 52 and 59 of the Treaty and Council Directive 77/62/EEC as amended by 88/295/EEC (the Supplies Directive, as it was then). Italy argued that the case was to be distinguished from Case 3/88 *Commission v. Italy* [1989] ECR 4035, [1991] 2 CMLR 115 in that it was related not to a sale of goods, but to a concession, amounting to a transfer of the right to conduct the lottery. Italy also represented that it was not a service contract either, although that was perhaps an unnecessary averment because the Services Directive had not yet come into force. In response to these submissions the Court remarked that it was still the State that awarded the prize, and there was no transfer of responsibility for the lottery, although the contract involved the supply of everything necessary to conduct the lottery. Therefore the derogation in paragraph 1 of article 55 of the Treaty, regarding activities connected with the exercise of official authority, did not apply. The fact that the system was not to become the property of the State until the end of the contract period, and that the price was to take the form of an annual payment in proportion to revenue, did not make it any less a public supply contract within the terms of the Directive.

The Commission also argued that the concession contract was in breach of article 30 of the Treaty. They relied on C-21/88 *Du Pont de Nemours* v. *Carrara Health Authority* [1990] ECR I-889, [1991] 3 CMLR 25, which says that article 30 precludes national rules that reserve a proportion of public supply contracts to undertakings that have production units in certain parts of national territory. But the Court declared that contention inadmissible, because it could not be said that the goods supplied by the company that was awarded the lottery concession would necessarily come only from Italy.

Competition

Articles 85 and 86 of the EC Treaty prohibit cartels, anti-competitive agreements, and other kinds of exploitation and unfair competition within the European Community. Their relevance to public procurement is that they prevent arrangements either by buyers or sellers which artificially restrict the market. The articles read as follows:

- *Article 85*

  1 The following shall be prohibited as incompatible with the common market: all agreements between undertakings, decisions by associations of undertakings and concerted practices which may affect trade between Member States and which have as their object or effect the prevention restriction or distortion of competition within the common market, and in particular those which:

  (a) directly or indirectly fix purchase or selling prices or any other trading conditions;
  (b) limit or control production, markets, technical development, or investment;
  (c) share markets or sources of supply;
  (d) apply dissimilar conditions to equivalent transactions with other trading parties, thereby placing them at a competitive disadvantage;
  (e) make the conclusion of contracts subject to acceptance by other parties of supplementary obligations which, by their nature or according to commercial usage, have no connection with the subject matter of such contracts.

  2 Any agreements or decisions prohibited pursuant to this Article shall be automatically void.

  3 The provisions of Paragraph 1 may, however, be declared inapplicable in the case of:

  - any agreement or category of agreement between undertakings;
  - any decisions or category of decisions by associations of undertakings;
  - any concerted practice or category of concerted practices;

  which contributes to improving the production or distribution of goods or to promoting technical or economic progress, while allowing consumers a fair share of the resulting benefit, and which does not:

(a) impose on the undertakings concerned restrictions which are not indispensable to the attainment of these objectives;

(b) afford such undertakings the possibility of eliminating competition in respect of a substantial part of the products in question.

- *Article 86*

Any abuse by one or more undertakings of a dominant position within the common market or in a substantial part of it shall be prohibited as incompatible with the common market in so far as it may affect trade between the Member States.

Such abuse may, in particular, consist in:

(a) directly or indirectly imposing unfair purchase or selling prices or other unfair trading conditions;

(b) limiting production, markets or technical development to the prejudice of consumers;

(c) applying dissimilar conditions to equivalent transactions with other trading parties, thereby placing them at a competitive disadvantage;

(d) making the conclusion of contracts subject to the acceptance by the other parties of supplementary obligations which, by their nature or according to commercial usage, have no connection with the subject of such contracts.

All agreements within the scope of article 85 must be notified to the Commission. Agreements falling within article 85(1) are automatically void, and the prohibition is wide, extending to market sharing, and price fixing between suppliers. The Commission has wide powers of investigation into these kinds of dealings. Under EC Regulation 17 (OJ Sp Ed 1959-62 p87) the officials of the Commission can arm themselves with a decision ordering a company to submit to an investigation, and a company can be heavily fined for failing to produce records or refusing to submit to an investigation, quite apart from the penalty that can be exacted for the breach of article 85. The impact upon procurement extends to joint procurement, joint bidding and joint execution of work, collaboration agreements, or teaming agreements. Such arrangement may be subject to European competition law.

There is no reason why a bid for a contract should be made by a natural or legal person. Groupings of suppliers, contractors or service providers can tender or negotiate for contracts, but if awarded the contract they may then be required to take on a specific legal form (see, for example, article 33 of Council Directive 93/38/EEC, the Utilities Directive). One legal form specifically devised by the Commission to facilitate cross-border cooperation between enterprises within the European Union is the European Economic Interest Grouping (EEIG), described in Council Regulation 2137/85/EEC (OJ L199 31.7.85 p1) and implemented by the European Economic Interest Groupings Regulations (SI 1989/638). If a joint venture, whether by means of an EEIG or otherwise, is proposed the parties should be aware of the Merger Regulation, 4064/89/EEC (OJ L257 21.9.90 p14), Commission Regulation 3384/94 (OJ L377 31.12.94), which covers procedure, the Commission Notice on Concentrative and Cooperative Operations under the Merger Regulation (OJ C203 14.8.90 p5), and the Commission Notice on Assessment of Cooperative Joint Ventures under Article 85 (OJ C43 16.2.93 p2). The Merger Regulation gives the Commission the power to control the growth of conglomerates. It applies to large concentrations with a Community dimension: that is to say, where the combined aggregate worldwide turnover of all the undertakings concerned is more than 5000 million ECU and the aggregate Community-wide turnover of at least two of the undertakings concerned is more than 250 million ECU, unless each of the undertakings concerned achieves more than two-thirds of its aggregate Community-wide turnover within one and the same Member State. A cooperative joint venture does not constitute a concentration for the purposes of the Merger Regulation, if the object is the coordination of the competitive behaviour of undertakings that remain independent, but if the joint venture is calculated to perform autonomously, as an economic unit, on a lasting basis, it may be characterised as concentrative, and thus will fall within the scope of the Regulation (see article 3). A joint venture that is not concentrative may still offend against article 85 of the Treaty.

Any agreement that is contrary to the terms of article 85, is automatically void; a 'gentlemen's agreement' suffices if it amounts to a concerted practice. It does not even matter that the company concerned is not in the European Union: see the *Dye-stuffs Case*, Case 48/69 *ICI* v. *Commission* [1972] ECR 619, [1972] CMLR 557. The agreement must affect trade between Member States, but an agreement confined in effect to a single Member State will be held to have this consequence if it results in an exclusive hold over the entire territory of a Member State, as happened in, for example, Case 8/72 *Cementhandelaren* [1972] ECR 977, [1973] CMLR 7, which was about an arrangement between cement manufacturers to tie up the market for cement in the Netherlands.

Minor agreements are beneath the Commission's notice: see Commission Notice on Minor Agreements (OJ C 231 12.9.86 p2); this relates to agreements for less than 5% of total market and where aggregate turnover does not exceed 200 million ECU.

Exemptions

Agreements within the scope of article 85 have to be notified to the Commission. It is possible to apply for exemption or negative clearance: that is to say, exemption for article 85 or a certificate that the agreement does not come within the article anyway. Regulation 17 (OJ Sp Ed 1959-62 p87) governs the procedure for applying for exemption and negative clearance. There is a system of block exemptions, set out in a number of regulations, to cover certain kinds of agreement that are commonly met. The block exemptions simply obviate the need to make individual applications for exemption: exclusive distribution agreements, Commission Regulation 1983/83 (OJ L173 30.6.83 p1); exclusive purchasing, Commission Regulation 1984/83 (OJ L173 30.6.83 p5); specialisation agreements, Commission Regulation 417/85 (OJ L53 22.2.85 p1); research and development agreements, Commission Regulation 418/85 (OJ L53 22.2.85 p5); franchising, Commission Regulation 4087/88 (OJ L359 28.12.88 p46); motor vehicle distribution and servicing, Commission Regulation 1475/95 (OJ L145 29.6.95 p25); and technology transfer, Commission Regulation 240/96 (OJ L131 9.2.96 p2).

Regulation 17 is implemented by Commission Regulation 3385/94 of 21 December 1994 on the form, content and other details of applications and notifications provided for in Council Regulation number 17; it replaces the old Regulation 27. Applications for negative clearance, notification of agreements, and exemption must be made by sending detailed information to the Commission on form A/B. Explanatory notes are set out in the appendix to Regulation 3385/94 (OJ L377 31.12.94 p28).

Hearings

Decisions made by the Commission in relation to competition matters are subject to review. A procedure for hearings is set out in Regulation 99/63 (OJ Sp Ed 1963-4 p47), whereby the Commission sends a statement of objections, the company can file a reply, and there is a hearing. Appeal lies to the Court of First Instance and thence to the European Court.

Abuse of a dominant position

Article 86 concerns unfair conduct by undertakings who have obtained a dominant position in the market. Utilities may obtain the 40–45% share of the relevant market considered by the Commission to indicate market dominance, and are thus affected, and some suppliers may hold such a strong position in the market that they are able to exclude their competitors from bidding effectively for public contracts. In the United Brands case, Case 6/72 *Europemballage Corporation and Continental Can Company Inc v. EC Commission* [1979] ECR 215, [1973] CMLR 199, 'dominance' was defined as a position of economic strength enjoyed by an undertaking that enables it to hinder the maintenance of effective competition on the relevant market by allowing it to behave to an appreciable extent independently of its competitors and customers. Abuse of such a position may be exclusionary, such as predatory pricing, loyalty rebates and refusal to supply, or exploitative, such as charging unfairly high prices.

The legislative framework

In order to tackle the law of public purchasing the reader must have to hand the four main Purchasing Directives, the two

Remedies Directives, and four sets of Statutory Instruments, namely the Supplies Regulations, the Works Regulations, the Services Regulations and the Utilities Regulations. No European regulations have been made in relation to public purchasing, so that there will be no confusion in this book if we refer to the United Kingdom legislation as 'the Regulations' and to the EC legislation as 'the Directives'. We shall first consider the history of the Directives, and then consider how they have been implemented by the Regulations.

The Directives

There are three directives for the public sector, concerned with the procedures to be used when placing contracts for, respectively, public works, supplies, and services in that sector.

The Works Directive used to be Council Directive 71/305/EEC of 26 July 1971 concerning the coordination of procedures for the award of public works contracts (OJ L185 16.8.71 p5), but this, having undergone substantial amendments, the major amendment being Council Directive 89/440/EEC (OJ L210 21.7.89 p1), was finally consolidated into Directive 93/37/EEC (OJ L199 9.8.93 p54). The latter is a purely consolidating measure.

The Supplies Directive used to be Council Directive 77/62 of 21 December 1976 coordinating procedures for the award of public supply contracts (OJ L13 15.1.77 p1), but this has now been completely superseded by Council Directive 93/36/EEC of 14 June 1993, a directive that not only consolidates many earlier amendments, but also makes changes designed to improve the clarity of the existing provisions. The date for implementation of this consolidating directive was 14 June 1994.

The Services Directive is Council Directive 92/50/EEC of 18 June 1992 relating to the coordination of procedures for the award of public service contracts (OJ L209 24.7.92 p1); this had to be implemented by 1 July 1993.

For the private sector there is but one directive, commonly known as the Utilities Directive, relating to procedures for the award of contracts for the purchase of supplies, services and works by the utilities. The full title of the directive is Council Directive 93/38/EEC coordinating the procurement procedures of entities operating in the water, energy, transport and tele-communications sectors (OJ L199 9.8.93 p84). The implementation date for this directive, which is a consolidating measure replacing Council Directive 90/531 of 17 September 1990 (OJ L297 29.10.90 p1), was 1 July 1994.

There are two Remedies Directives, that is to say directives enforcing compliance with purchasing procedures, and *inter alia* requiring Member States to create procedures whereby suppliers, or would-be suppliers, may have redress for their grievances. In the public sector, compliance with the Supplies and Works and Services Directives is enforced by Council Directive 89/665/EEC of 21 December 1989 on the coordination of the laws, regulations and administrative provisions relating to the application of review procedures to the award of public supply and public works contracts (OJ L395 30.12.89 p33); this is commonly called the Compliance Directive. In the private sector, compliance with the Utilities Directive is enforced by Council Directive 92/13/EEC of 25 February 1992 coordinating the laws, regulations and administrative provisions relating to the application of community rules on the procurement procedures of entities operating in the water, energy, transport and tele-communications sectors (OJ L76 23.3.92 p14); this is usually called the Remedies Directive.

The Regulations

The Directives are implemented in the United Kingdom by a series of regulations. The Public Works Contracts Regulations 1991 (SI 1991/2680) implement the Works Directive, 93/37/EEC, and, to the extent that it relates to that directive, the corresponding Compliance Directive, 89/665/EEC. The Public Supply Contracts Regulations 1991 (SI 1991/2679) implement the Supplies Directive, 93/36/EEC, and, to the extent that it relates to that directive, the corresponding Compliance Directive, 89/665/EEC. And the Public Services Contracts Regulations 1993 (SI 1993/3228) implement the Services Directive, 92/50/EEC, and contain compliance provisions identical to those in the other directives.

The Utilities Supply and Works Contracts Regulations 1992 (SI 1992/3279) implement, except with regard to services contracts, the Utilities Directive, 93/38/EEC, and the corresponding Remedies Directive, 92/13/EEC. At the time of writing further legislation remained to be enacted in order to implement the recent consolidation of the Utilities Directive, and the consequent addition of services contracts to that directive. At the time of writing the new regulations had not been made, and until they are it is necessary to refer to the Directive whenever a services contract is considered.

It is important to know what principles govern the interpretation of these regulations, and what is to happen if it be found that the European law is either not implemented (as was the case for the Utilities Directive at the time of writing) or not implemented correctly. The rule is that where the provisions of a directive appear, as far as the subject matter is concerned, to be unconditional and sufficiently precise, those provisions may be relied on by individuals against the State where the State fails to implement the directive in national law within the period prescribed, or where it fails to implement the directive correctly. It will always be possible to rely upon this doctrine against a contracting authority or utility, because these bodies will always be emanations of the State. To understand the doctrine in the context of public purchasing it is useful to consider Case 31/87 *Gebroeders Beentjes NV* v. *Netherlands* [1988] ECR 4635, [1990] 1 CMLR 287. This was a case where Beentjes BV claimed damages from the Netherlands government on the basis that, although it had submitted the lowest bid, it had not been awarded a public works contract by the Waterland Local Land Consolidation Committee. A question arose on whether the criterion of the most acceptable tender as laid down in the legislation of the Netherlands was compatible with the Works Directive. It was said that it was the duty of a Member State, under article 5 of the Treaty, to take all appropriate measures to achieve the result envisaged by a directive. It followed that in applying national law, in particular provisions of national law specifically introduced in order to implement a directive, national courts are required to interpret their national law in the light of the wording and purpose of the directive in order to achieve the result referred to in the third paragraph of article 189 of the Treaty, namely that a directive 'shall be binding as to the result to be achieved'.

Summary

The structure of each of the Regulations is the same: Part I deals with interpretation, definitions and thresholds; Part II with technical specifications; Part III with procedures, notices, timetables and choice of procedure; Part IV with the selection of suppliers; Part V with the award; Part VI with miscellaneous matters such as the dispatch of notices and the provision of information; and Part VII with applications to the Court.

The following table shows the various directives and the corresponding implementing legislation as it stood in August 1996:

EC directives	UK implementing legislation
The Works Directive 93/97 and the Compliance Directive 89/665	The Public Works Contracts Regulations SI (1991) 2680
The Supplies Directive 93/36 and the Compliance Directive 89/665	The Public Supply Contracts Regulations SI (1995) 201
The Services Directive 92/50 and the Compliance Directive 89/665	The Public Services Contracts Regulations SI (1993) 3228
The Utilities Directive 93/38 and the Remedies Directive 93/13	The Utilities Supply and Works Contracts Regulations SI (1992) 3279

Supply chain management

Before he attempts to understand what the Purchasing Directives do, the lawyer should consider what is meant by the term *procurement*. It embraces the whole process of acquisition from third parties, a process sometimes referred to as *supply chain management*, and covers goods, services and construction projects. The professional buyer undertakes this task in a systematic way. He first defines his business need, and for this purpose he must understand the capacity of the market, and the extent of competition for the supply. He then determines what strategy to employ, invites tenders, evaluates them, refines them, awards the contract, operates and manages it, monitors performance, and uses his knowledge so gained as a basis for further purchasing decisions. The Purchasing Directives are not designed to make this process any easier. They are there for economic reasons, to make the process more transparent, obliging purchasers to record and account for their actions to a court if necessary. This is why the Directives contain strict requirements as to the publication of notices in the *Official Journal*, as to the choice of procedures leading to the award of a contract, and as to the criteria for making the award. The buyer is obliged to work within this framework, but his chief concern is not to be fair, but rather to obtain the right quality, in the right quantity, from the right source, delivered to the right place, at the right time, and at the right price.

A lawyer might think that the fairest way to place a contract would be to put it out to open tender, but in practice this is usually impracticable. An open tender involves the preparation of identical specifications, which must be issued to each prospective contractor. Each tenderer must submit his bid in a sealed envelope by a prescribed date. The bids must be kept safe in their envelopes until the due date. They are then opened and tenders evaluated, which means that an assessment is made of whether the tenderer can fulfil the contract, whether his bid meets the specification, whether he can meet appropriate quality standards, and whether all the costs and other financial criteria of the contract are addressed.

It is easy to see why this system is usually inappropriate. If many contractors bid then much money and time is wasted in assessing the bids. In the case of a large engineering project the specifications will be voluminous and complicated. If many are called but few chosen the process is expensive, not only to the buyer, but also to the bidder.

Instead of open bidding some prequalification process is usually used, to screen prospective bidders so that a shortlist of those with the capacity to perform the contract can be invited to tender. The object is to reduce numbers, not to reduce competition. The most suitable supplier will be the one who will give the best value for money. In the public sector, value for money is achieved when a public body carries out its duties to a high standard at a low cost: that is, when its administration and the service it provides is economic, efficient and effective.

Economy, efficiency and effectiveness are interrelated. A body cannot be efficient and uneconomic, but it can be cheap and tawdry. Though efficient it may be ineffective, if ill directed. Therefore the most suitable supplier will be the one most commercially and technically capable, financially sound, keen to obtain and agree the contract on value for money terms, and likely to carry it out efficiently.

If his purchase is to be effective the buyer must ensure that it is directed towards a real need. This is not always easy. If he is buying a computer system, to take the most obvious example, he may not know what he wants – may not even know that he does not know. It will be no satisfaction to him if he binds himself to award a contract to the supplier who precisely meets his specification, only to discover that the task can be performed more effectively in entirely another way. Therefore the buyer will spend time on the preparation of documentation for the contract. The specification is the key document, defining what the purchaser wants to buy, neither too broad nor too narrow, but containing the right quality and performance standards. The Procurement Directives oblige the buyer to use European standards, or equivalent, whenever possible, so that suppliers from other Member States will not be dissuaded from bidding.

The Purchasing Directives oblige the buyer to advertise his requirements in the *Official Journal*, provided that the contract is worth more than the relevant threshold value (the thresholds are tabulated in Chapter 2). If the buyer chooses to put out the contract to open tender he is said, in the terminology of the Directives, to use an *open procedure*. If only a shortlist of candidates are entitled to bid, he uses a *restricted procedure*. If he simply chooses the persons with whom he wishes to negotiate, he is said to use the *negotiated procedure*.

The buyer will choose the bid, or negotiate an offer, which appears to him to represent the best overall value for money. The criteria he uses in making this judgment, and their relative order of importance, must be determined before anyone is invited to bid, and must not be changed afterwards. Quite apart from the

Directives, it would be unethical to accept a bid on some other basis. If, for example, a competitor could offer the lowest price, but was constrained to provide a particular quality, he would have a legitimate complaint if the contract were to be placed on the basis of price alone. The Purchasing Directives reflect these ethical considerations in that, unless the lowest price is the only criterion, those criteria that are to be applied in selecting a tender must appear in the contractual documentation.

The Directives provide that an award can be made only on the basis of either the lowest price or the most economically advantageous tender. These bases for the award of a contract are known as the *award criteria*. Whether a tender is economically advantageous involves consideration of various criteria, such as: delivery or completion date, running costs, cost-effectiveness, quality, aesthetic and functional characteristics, technical merit, after-sales service and technical assistance, commitments with regard to spare parts, security of supplies, and price.

Whatever the quality of the bid, the purchaser will want to investigate the quality of the bidder. If the order is of any importance the buyer will check that the supplier has the capacity, capability, commitment and financial viability to meet the requirements of the contract. This process, known as *supplier appraisal*, might involve examining the supplier's balance sheets, visiting the factory to see if the employees are busy and well organised or lazy and muddled, investigating labour relations, and considering the location and accessibility of the factory. Supplier appraisal involves issuing questionnaires, asking for bank references, and carrying out other kinds of investigation.

All the Public Sector Directives, under the heading of 'Criteria for qualitative selection', contain rules on who may be excluded from participation in a contract, and rules on the kind of evidence of capability and capacity to perform it that may be demanded. A supplier who, for example, is bankrupt or being wound up can be excluded from the tendering process. Contracting authorities must specify in the contract notice or invitation to tender what bank references and other evidence the supplier must provide as proof of financial and economic standing. And there is a list of the kind of information, such as (in the case of a works contract) a list of works carried out over the past five years, that a purchaser may require a contractor to furnish in order to demonstrate his technical capability.

After the contract has been placed the buyer will evaluate the performance of the supplier; this evaluation of how well a supplier performs the contract is called *vendor rating,* and it is related to the general process of vendor appraisal. The object of having a system of vendor rating is to measure the relative performance of suppliers by measuring their scores on delivery, service, quality, price and other factors.

A buyer in the private sector sees his suppliers as a resource of cash, machinery and manpower. A company will take as much care in selecting its suppliers as it does the selection of its finance, equipment and personnel. Therefore the Utilities Directive allows for the use of more flexible procedures than are to be found in the public sector. In the private sector the use of the negotiated procedure is not exceptional. The utilities are permitted to operate a system of prequalification, involving the compilation of approved lists of their suppliers. The system must be based on objective criteria, and must be made available to interested suppliers on request.

The Purchasing Directives contain much that sensible buyers would consider common sense. But to make rules of law out of a half-understood appreciation of what buyers do is not a way to make good law. The Directives are difficult to understand, of doubtful effect, over-prescriptive, and for the most part unnecessary; a system of inspection and attestation would have been better.

Chapter 2

Common Features

In this chapter we shall consider the common features of the Purchasing Directives. In later chapters of this book we consider each of the implementing regulations. Because of the way in which the Directives have been drafted it is not possible to avoid a certain amount of repetition. The reader must first grasp the general scheme of the Directives, but whenever a problem arises he must abandon generalities and study the individual regulation and corresponding directive because there are many irritating differences in detail.

The Commission could have adopted a single directive for all kinds of public purchasing, but chose not to do so because it was difficult to compose a composite creature that would cater for the different features of different kinds of contract. The legislation has developed piecemeal, and there are now three separate directives dealing with works, supplies and services contracts in the public sector. When the Utilities Directive was introduced the draftsmen were sufficiently brave to formulate a single directive covering the purchasing of supplies, services (by later amendment), and works in the private sector. The Utilities Directive conforms the least, because greater latitude has been given to private sector enterprises to adopt commercial methods of buying.

The Directives reflect good buying practice, but they are not designed to achieve efficient management or commercial advantage. They have social and economic aims: that is, the opening up of public contracts to Europe-wide competition, with the consequent savings that this will entail, and the achievement of transparency in the buying process so that suppliers will be able to see how decisions were made and why a particular tender was rejected or accepted. The Directives endeavour to achieve this by several means: the advertising of contracts above a certain threshold value throughout the European Union so that contractors in every Member State will have an equal opportunity to tender; the prohibition of technical specifications that might favour particular contractors; and the application of objective criteria for the selection of suppliers and the award of contracts.

Application

One or other of the Directives will apply whenever a utility or contracting authority seeks offers in relation to a proposed contract, other than one excluded from the Directives.

Each directive is supposed to be a self-contained code. Sometimes it is difficult to establish which directive applies, but a contract is never subject to more than one directive.

If a public sector contract is intended to cover both supplies and services it falls within the scope of the Services Directive if the value of the services in question exceeds that of the products covered by the contract (see article 2 of the Directive). *Supply* includes siting or installation (see regulation 2 of the Supplies Regulations).

A contract is subject to the Works Directive if it has as its object either the execution, or both the execution and design, of works related to one of the activities referred to in Annex II of that directive. The annex contains a list of professional activities as set out in the General Industrial Classification of Economic Activities within the European Community (NACE). The Works Directive also applies to contracts for a *work*, which is defined as 'the outcome of building or civil engineering works taken as a whole that is sufficient of itself to fulfil an economic and technical function'.

If the purchasing entity is a utility, then the Utilities Directive applies. When a public authority carries out one of the activities listed in article 2 of the Utilities Directive, for example the operation of a fixed network intended to provide a service to the public in connection with the distribution of drinking water, electricity, gas, or heat, it will be subject to the Utilities Directive. The result is that a local authority may find that it is subject both to the Directives for the public sector and to the Utilities directive.

Territorial scope

The Directives apply to contractors who are nationals of and established in a Relevant State. The procurement regime extends not only to the European Union but also to States within the European Economic Area and States connected to the European Union by various Europe agreements. At the time of writing the Relevant States were:

- European Union Member States
- Norway
- Iceland
- Liechtenstein
- Hungary
- Poland

Contracting authorities

In the public sector the Purchasing Directives apply to contracts placed by 'contracting authorities'. In article 1 of each of the Directives a *contracting authority* is defined as: '...the State, regional or local authorities, bodies governed by public law, associations formed by one or several such authorities or bodies governed by public law'. What is important to this definition is the existence of State control or influence. Thus a 'body governed by public law' (a novel concept as far as the common law is concerned) is defined as a body established for the specific purpose of meeting needs in the general interest, not having an industrial or commercial character, having legal personality, and financed, for the most part, by the State, or regional or local authorities, or other bodies governed by public law; or subject to management supervision by those bodies; or having an administrative, managerial or supervisory board, more than half of whose members are appointed by the state, regional or local authorities or by other bodies governed by public law.

Lists of bodies, or of categories of bodies, governed by public law, which fulfil the above criteria, are set out in annex I to the Works Directive 93/37/EEC. These lists are supposed to be as exhaustive as possible, and may be reviewed in accordance with the procedure laid down in article 35 of that directive, but the lists are not definitive. Reference should also be made to regulation 3 of each of the Regulations, where the contracting authorities for the purposes of the Regulations are defined and listed.

The nature of the entities affected by the Directives was discussed in Case 31/87 *Gebroeders Beentjes NV* v. *Netherlands* [1988] ECR 4635, [1990] 1 CMLR 287. This case concerned the interpretation of the Works Directive and its application to the Waterland Local Land Consolidation Committee. It was said that a body whose composition and functions are laid down by legislation and which depends on the authorities for the appointment of its members, the observance of obligations arising out of its measures, and the financing of public works contracts which it is its task to award, must be regarded as falling within the notion of the State for the purposes of article 1 of the Works Directive so that the Directive applies to the contracts that it awards.

Utilities

The Utilities Directive uses the term *contracting entity* to denote those bodies to which the Directive will apply, namely those public authorities or undertakings that exercise one of the activities set out in article 2(2) of the Directive, and contracting entities that are not public authorities or public undertakings that have as one of their activities any of those referred to in article 2(2) or any combination thereof and operate on the basis of special or exclusive rights granted by a competent authority of a Member State. A utility is thus defined by reference to its function rather than its form. The activities referred to cover four kinds of activity. The first kind of activity is the provision or operation of fixed networks intended to provide a service to the public in connection with the production, transport or distribution of drinking water, or electricity, or gas or heat; or the supply of drinking water, electricity, gas or heat to such networks. The second kind is the exploitation of a geographical area for the purpose of exploring for or extracting oil, gas, coal or other solid fuels; or for the provision of airport, maritime or inland port or other terminal facilities to carriers by air, sea or inland waterway. The third kind is the operation of networks providing a service to the public in the field of transport by railway, automated systems, tramway, trolley bus, bus or cable. The fourth kind is the provision or operation of public telecommunications networks, or the provision of one or more public telecommunications services.

The draftsman of the Utilities Regulations, in an effort to simplify these provisions, has set out the relevant utilities in a schedule to the Regulations. The schedule contains two columns, one naming the relevant utilities and the other describing the corresponding relevant activities. The schedule caters for the fact that certain activities, for example the production of gas or heat as an unavoidable consequence of activities that do not fall within article 2 and its supply (not more than 20% of turnover) to a public network, are not treated as relevant activities.

Contracts covered

Public works contracts are defined in article 1 of the Works Directive as contracts for pecuniary interest concluded in writing between a contractor and a contracting authority, which have as their object 'either the execution, or both the execution and design, of works related to one of the activities referred to in Annex II or a work'. A *work* is defined as the outcome of building or civil engineering works taken as a whole that is sufficient of itself to fulfil an economic and technical function. This distinction between work and works is important in relation to the aggregation rules, because it is the value of the work rather than the component works that determines, in many cases, whether the contract exceeds the relevant threshold.

Public service contracts mean contracts for pecuniary interest concluded in writing between a service provider and a contracting authority. *Public supply contracts* are contracts for pecuniary interest concluded in writing involving the purchase, lease rental or hire purchase, with or without option to buy, of products between a supplier and a contracting authority.

It is clear from the scheme of the Directives that they are not to be avoided merely by refraining from writing, because they are read purposively. Some questions may arise as to what is a 'contract'. If a local authority accepts an in-house bid there is no contract, but it would be wrong in such circumstances to assume that the Directives had no effect. The Directives are concerned with the process of awarding contracts, not the end result. The unfair award of a contract in house would inevitably involve a breach of the Directives at some stage in the process, or if not that then a breach of the implementing regulations. In *R* v. *Portsmouth City Council* ex parte *Coles*, The Times, 13 November 1996, a local authority failed to set out the award criteria in either the contract documents or the invitations to tender for several of its works contracts. This omission was clearly a breach of the Works Directive, but in judicial review proceedings the council argued that where work was awarded to its direct labour organisation the council could not have been awarding a contract properly so called, because it was not possible for the council to contract with its own department. The Court of Appeal held that argument to be correct, but went on to say that where the Works Regulations (SI 1991/2680) applied the obvious lacuna in the Works Directive was made good by regulation 20(8), which states that for the purposes of the regulation an offer includes a bid by one part of a contracting authority to carry out work or works by another part of the contracting authority.

Framework agreements

A framework agreement is an arrangement (not necessarily a contract) whereby a supplier or service provider undertakes to provide goods or services, up to a certain amount, over a given period of time, and at a certain price. Under article 5 of the Utilities Directive contracting entities may regard a framework agreeement as if it were a contract, and award it in accordance with the Directive. A prior call for competition is not necessary if a contract is awarded under a framework agreement. The Public Sector Directives contain no specific provision for framework agreements; however, the Commission has approved such arrangements, and individual call-offs do not need to be advertised if they lie below the relevant threshold. In Case C-79/94 *Commission* v. *Greece* [1995] ECR I-1071, [1996] 2 CMLR 134, the European Court considered a framework agreement under which individual supply contracts were below the relevant threshold. It held that the framework agreement should have been advertised, in accordance with the Supplies Directive, because the total value of the contracts did exceed the threshold.

General exclusion

Each of the Directives contains a list of exclusions. In each case it is necessary to examine in detail the list of exclusions for a particular directive, but some matters are common to all the Directives. The exclusion of defence contracts, except those to which article 223 of the EC Treaty applies, and secret or security contracts is common to all the Directives. The Directives are also mutually exclusive, in the sense that no contract can be subject to the regime of more than one Directive. None of the Directives applies to contracts governed by different international procedural rules, pursuant to international agreements, relating to stationing of troops, or pursuant to particular procedures of international organisations. Contracts worth less than certain threshold values, which vary according to the type of contract, are automatically excluded.

Thresholds

In order to calculate the value of a contract one takes, as a general rule, the estimated value of the contract (net of value added tax) at the relevant time: that is, the time when the contract notice is sent to the *Official Journal*. It is forbidden to split a contract into parts in order to avoid the threshold, and if, for example, a contracting authority has a requirement over a period for goods of the type to be purchased or hired under a public supply contract and for that purpose enters into a series of contracts or a contract that under its terms is renewable, then there are rules, commonly known as *aggregation*, under which the value of the contract is calculated by reference to the consideration given over a period of 12 months; see the Public Supply Contracts Regulations 1995, regulation 7.

In January 1995 the thresholds were changed to take account of the terms of the Government Purchasing Agreement, as to which see Chapter 1. In order to avoid the difficulties that would arise if each Member State had to recalculate the value of the thresholds in line with exchange rates each time it placed a contract, the Commission should publish every two years a notice giving the value of the relevant thresholds in national currencies. The values given in this book are derived from an informal Commission circular, and the amendments to the Directives were, at the time of writing, still in draft form.

The table below gives not only the thresholds at which the Directives become operative, but also the threshold for the prior information notice, or indicative notice. A contracting authority must as soon as possible after the commencement of each financial year send a prior information notice to the *Official Journal* with, at the date of dispatch of the notice, the total consideration that the contracting authority expects to give under (for example) all the proposed public supply contracts that are for the purchase or hire of goods falling within the same product area equals or exceeds the relevant threshold.

A few words of explanation are necessary for those who have yet to understand the terminology and system of the Directives. The first table sets out the thresholds that apply to those central government purchasing authorities that are subject to the Government Purchasing Agreement. In Schedule 2 of the Supplies Regulations (SI 1995/201) there is a list of these central government contracting authorities, who were subject to GATT, and are now subject to its successor, the World Trade Organisation Agreement on Government Purchasing (WTO, GPA). Purchasing of supplies and services by these authorities is generally subject to lower thresholds than those applied elsewhere, and these are based upon Standard Drawing Rights (SDRs) as a result of the GPA.

Research and development (R&D) contracts do not come

within the GPA, and therefore the higher EU threshold always applies. R&D services come within the scope of the Directives only where the benefits accrue exclusively to the contracting authority/utility for its use in the conduct of its own affairs and are wholly paid for by the contracting entity.

The Services Regulations and Directive, and the Utilities Directive, contain a schedule setting out those services to which the regime of the Directives appertains. The full regime of the Services Directive applies to those services set out in part A of the schedule. Those services listed in part B of the schedule are commonly called *residual services*, and to these services only the requirements relating to specifications and standards, and certain reporting requirements apply. Residual services are not included in the GPA, and therefore the higher EU threshold always applies to these services.

As to the term *indicative notice*, this means the annual notice that a purchasing entity has to publish each year to indicate its requirement for the following year. It is also called a *prior information notice*.

The reference to 'small lots' is to the provisions under, for example, regulation 7(4) of the Works Regulations. Normally, for the purposes of calculating the threshold, a contract that is one of several entered into for the purpose of carrying out a work is taken to be worth the aggregate of all the contracts for carrying out the work. A derogation applies if the contract has a value of less than 1,000,000 ECU, and the aggregate value of that contract, and any other contract for the carrying out of the work in respect of which the contracting authority takes advantage of the derogation, is less than 20% of the aggregate value of the consideration that the contracting authority will pay under all the contracts for carrying out the work. This is explained further in Chapter 6.

Some utilities are now subject to the WTO Government Procurement Agreement, but the EU threshold is marginally lower than the GPA threshold, and therefore the EU threshold applies to these entities.

Under the Utilities Directive there is a separate higher threshold in the telecommunications sector.

Also mentioned in the list below is the IT standards threshold. This threshold is set by Council Decision of 22 December 1986 on

standardisation in the field of information technology and telecommunications 87/95/EEC (OJ L36 7.2.87 p31), and requires
the use of the open standards set out in that Decision in the case
of contracts above the threshold.

Table of thresholds

(1) Purchasing by authorities subject to the GPA (Central
Government Purchases)

Supplies	£108,667	(130,000 SDR)
Services	£108,667	(130,000 SDR)
R & D services	£158,018	(200,000 ECU)
Residual services	£158,018	(200,000 ECU)
Indicative notices for supplies/services	£592,568	(750,000 ECU)
Small lots for services contracts	£63,207	(80,000 ECU)
Works contracts	£3,950,456	(5,000,000 ECU)
Small lots for works contracts	£790,091	(1,000,000 ECU)
Subject to IT standards decision	£79,000	(100,000 ECU)

(2) Other public sector purchasing authorities (sub-central
government)

Supplies	£158,018	(200,000 ECU)
Services	£158,018	(200,000 ECU)
R & D services	£158,018	(200,000 ECU)
Residual services	£158,018	(200,000 ECU)
Indicative notices for supplies/services	£592,568	(750,000 ECU)

Small lots for services contracts	£63,207	(80,000 ECU)
Works contracts	£3,950,456	(5,000,000 ECU)
Small lots for works contracts	£790,091	(1,000,000 ECU)
Subject to IT standards decision	£79,000	(100,000 ECU)

(3)   Utilities

Supplies – in the energy water and transport sectors	£316,036	(400,000 ECU)
Supplies – in the telecommunications sector	£474,055	(600,000 ECU)
Services – in the energy water and transport sectors	£316,036	(400,000 ECU)
Services – in the telecommunications sector	£474,055	(600,000 ECU)
Works	£3,950,456	(5,000,000 ECU)
Indicative notice for supplies	£592,568	(750,000 ECU)
Indicative notice for services	£592,568	(750,000 ECU)
Indicative notice for works	£3,950,456	(5,000,000 ECU)
Small lots for works	£790,091	(1,000,000 ECU)
Subject to IT standards decision	£79,000	(100,000 ECU)

Procedures

All of the Directives contain a requirement to send various notices to the *Official Journal of the European Communities*, and thereafter to follow a strict timetable for the consideration of bids. There are three procedures. Under the open procedure all interested suppliers, contractors or service providers may submit tenders. Under the restricted procedure, only candidates invited by the contracting entity may submit tenders. Under the negotiated procedure the contracting authority consults supplier, contractors or service providers of its choice and negotiates the terms of the contract with one or more of them. In the public sector the use of the negotiated procedure is limited to exceptional cases, when, for example, an emergency has arisen. In the private sector there is a freedom to use the negotiated procedure, but subject (as a rule) to satisfying a requirement for a call for competition.

Notices are published in the *Supplement* to the *Official Journal*. HMSO will provide individual copies of this Supplement, also any local Euro-Info Centre. The address of the Office of Official Publications of the European Communities, to which notices must be sent, is:

2 Rue Mercier,
L-2985 Luxembourg

Telex: 0402 1324 PUBOF LU
Fax: 00 352 49 00 03
Sales department telephone: 00 352 499 28 425 63

Where the authority is using the abridged time periods that are permitted in urgent cases, the notice must be sent by telex, telegram or facsimile, but there is no objection to using this method in ordinary cases. The notice must not contain more than 650 words. A record must be kept of the date of dispatch, and the authority must not place a notice in any other publication before that date; if it subsequently advertises in the local press it must not add information that was not sent to the *Official Journal*, save that it must mention the date it despatched the notice to the *Official Journal*.

There is no requirement to use any standard form, but there is a Commission Recommendation 91/561/EEC (OJ L305 16.11.91 p18) for the standardising of notices. Standard forms for use by public authorities are published in a special edition of the *Supplement* as an appendix to Commission Recommendation 91/561/EEC (OJ No S217 N 16.11.91 p1). A corresponding set of notices for utilities is also published (OJ No S252A 30.12.92). HMSO supplies forms for use by public authorities.

The TED database (Tenders Electronic Daily) publishes the notices on line. From 1995 TED has been available through national gateways, the gateway in the UK being known as Context Tenders. This database is the on-line version of the *Supplement* to the *Official Journal*. At the beginning of each notice a series of codes contains such information as the date of dispatch, name of the contracting entity, and type of award procedure used in the notice. For further information contact the Office of Official Publications of the EU.

Common Procurement Vocabulary

In order to describe the subject matter of contracts, in notices published in the *Official Journal*, contracting authorities and entities in both the public and private sector are recommended to use the Common Procurement Vocabulary (CPV).

The Commission recommendation 96/527/EEC (OJ L222 3.9.96 p10) states that the object of this vocabulary is to achieve administrative simplification. Each of the Procurement Directives requires the description of the subject matter of a contract to be given by reference to various nomenclatures: in the Services and Utilities Directives by reference to the Common Product Classification of the United Nations (CPC); in the Supplies Directive by reference to the Classification of Products by Activity (CPA); and in the Works and Utilities Directives by reference to the Statistical classification of economic activities in the European Community (NACE). It was felt urgently necessary to harmonise the references made to these different nomenclatures. Also, it was felt necessary to abandon the General Public Works Nomenclature, recommended hitherto by Commission Recommendation 91/561/EEC (OJ L305 6.11.91 p19).

The CPV is an adaptation of the Classification of Products by Activity (CPA) established by Council Regulation 3696/93/EEC (OJ L342 31.12.93 p1). The CPA offers a fixed correspondence with the CPC and comprises four digits of NACE Rev.1. The CPV is published as a supplement to the *Official Journal* (OJ S169 3.9.96 p1), and comprises a main vocabulary, supplementary vocabulary and an alphabetical index. Updates are distributed on the TED database. The use of the vocabulary will help to enable contract notices to be translated by computer. The code for potatoes is 01112100-6, and the code for nuclear thermal power stations is 45215122-8.

Time limits

The calculation of time limits is done in accordance with EC rules, and these are set out in Council Regulation (EEC Euratom) 1182/71 of 3 June 1971 determining the rules applicable to periods, dates and time limits (OJ L124 8.6.71 p1). The table following sets out the time limits that apply in respect of the various procedures under each of the Directives.

Tables of time limits

1. Supplies Regulations

Indicative notice (prior information notice)	As soon as possible after the commencement of the financial year

Open procedure

Open procedure notice	As soon as possible after forming the intention to seek offers in relation to a public supply contract
Last date for receipt of offers	Not less than 52 days from the date of dispatch of the notice. (This period should be extended if contract documents are too bulky to be supplied within 6 days of the request, or if further information would be supplied later than 6 days before the date for receipt of tenders, or if inspection of the site or other documents is necessary)

Contract documents to be sent	Within 6 days of receipt of request (provided they a requested in good time and any fee accompanies the request)
Further information	Must be supplied no later than 6 days before the date specified in the contract notice as the final date for the receipt of tenders

Restricted procedure

Notice	As soon as possible after forming the intention to seek offers in relation to a public supply contract
Last date for receipt of requests to tender	37 days from the date of dispatch of the notice (or not less than 15 days if 37 days is impractical for reasons of urgency)
Last date for the receipt of tenders	Not less than 40 days from the dispatch of the invitation. (This period must be extended if inspection of premises or documents is needed, and may be curtailed to not less than 10 days if 40 days is impractical for reasons of urgency)
Further information	Must be supplied not less than 6 days before the final date for receipt of tenders (provided that the request is received in sufficient time) but may be cutailed to not less than 4 days if 6 days is impractical for reasons of urgency

Negotiated procedure

Notice	As soon as possible after forming the intention to seek offers
Last date for receipt of requests to negotiate	Not less than 37 days from the date of dispatch of the notice (or not less than 15 days if 37 days is impractical for reasons of urgency)

All procedures

Contract award notice	No later than 48 days after the award
Information about contract award procedures	Within 15 days of the date on which the contracting authority receives a request from an unsuccessful supplier

2. Works Regulations

Indicative notice (prior information notice)	As soon as possible after the decision approving planning of the work or works

Open procedure

Notice	As soon as possible after forming the intention to seek offers in relation to a public works contract

Last date for receipt of tenders

Not less than 52 days (or 36 days when the authority has published a prior information notice) from the date of dispatch of the notice. (This period should be extended if contract documents are too bulky to be supplied within 6 days of the request, or if further information would be supplied later than 6 days before the date for receipt of tenders, or if inspection of the site or other documents is necessary)

Contract documents to be sent

Within 6 days of receipt of request, provided that the request is in good time and accompanied by fee

Further information

Must be supplied no later than 6 days before the date specified in the contract notice as the final date for the receipt of tenders (provided that the request is received in sufficient time) but this period may be curtailed to less than 4 days if 6 days is impractical for reasons of urgency

Restricted procedure

Notice

As soon as possible after forming the intention to seek offers in relation to a public works contract

Last date for receipt of requests to tender	Not less than 37 days from the date of dispatch of the notice (or, if this is impractical for reasons of urgency, not less than 15 days)
Last date for the receipt of tenders	Not less than 40 days (26 days if a prior information notice has been published) from the dispatch of the invitation. (This must be extended, if inspection of premises or supporting documents is needed, and may be curtailed to not less than 10 days if 40 days is impractical for reasons of urgency)
Further information	Must be supplied no later than 6 days before the date specified in the contract notice as the final date for the receipt of tenders (provided that the request is received in sufficient time) but this period may be curtailed to not less than 4 days if 6 days is impractical for reasons of urgency

Negotiated procedure

Negotiated procedure notice	As soon as possible after forming the intention to seek offers
Last date for receipt of requests to negotiate	Not less than 37 days from the date of dispatch of the notice (where impractical for reasons of urgency, not less than 15 days)

All procedures

Contract award notice	Not later than 48 days after the award
Information about contract award procedures	Within 15 days of the date on which the contracting authority receives a request from an unsuccessful contractor

Public works concession contracts

Contract notice	As soon as possible after forming intention
Final date for receipt of tenders or requests to be selected to tender or negotiate	Not less than 52 days from the date of dispatch of the notice

Concessionaire subcontracts

Final date for receipt of tenders	40 days from dispatch of notice
Final date for applications to be selected to tender or negotiate	37 days from dispatch of notice
Final date for receipt of tenders following selection of persons to be invited to tender	40 days from dispatch of invitation

3. Services Regulations

Prior information notice	As soon as possible after the commencement of each financial year

Open procedure

Notice	As soon as possible after forming the intention to seek offers in relation to a public services contract
Last date for receipt of offers	Not less than 52 days (36 days if a prior information notice has been published) from the date of dispatch of the notice. (This period should be extended if contract documents are too bulky to be supplied within 6 days of the request, or if further information would be supplied later than 6 days before the date for receipt of tenders, or if inspection of the site or other documents is necessary)
Contract documents to be sent	Within 6 days of receipt of request
Further information	Must be supplied no later than 6 days before the date specified in the contract notice as the final date for the receipt of tenders

Restricted procedure

Notice	As soon as possible after forming the intention to seek offers in relation to a public supply contract

Last date for receipt of requests to tender	37 days from the date of the dispatch of the notice (or, if 37 days is impractical for reasons of urgency, not less than 15 days)
Last date for the receipt of tenders	Not less than 40 days (26 days if a prior information notice has been published) from the dispatch of the invitation. (This period must be extended if inspection of the site or documents is needed, and may be curtailed to not less than 10 days if 40 days is impractical for reasons of urgency)
Further information	Must be sent not less than 6 days before the final date for receipt of tenders (provided that the request is received in sufficient time) but may be cutailed to not less than 4 days if 6 days is impractical for reasons of urgency

Negotiated procedure

Notice	As soon as possible after forming the intention to seek offers
Last date for receipt of requests to negotiate	Not less than 37 days from the date of dispatch of the notice (or not less than 15 days if 37 days is impractical for reasons of urgency)

All procedures

Contract award notice	No later than 48 days after the award

Information about contract award procedures	Within 15 days of the date on which the contracting authority receives a request from an unsuccessful supplier

Public service, competition

Award notice	No later than 48 days after the date jury has made its selection

4. The utilities

Indicative notice (prior information notice)	Must be published every 12 months. In order to satisfy a requirement for prior call for competition it must not be published more than 12 months prior to the invitation to suppliers/contractors/ service providers to express an interest

Open procedure

Notice	When required, there is no specific provision
Last date for receipt of offers	Not less than 52 days (36 days if an indicative notice was published) from the date of dispatch of the notice. (Account should be taken of the time required for examination of voluminous documentation or the need to inspect the site)
Contract documents to be sent	Within 6 days of receipt of request (provided requested in good time and accompanied by fee)

Further information	Must be supplied no later than 6 days before the final date for the receipt of tenders (provided requested in good time and accompanied by fee)

Restricted or negotiated procedures

(With call for competition)

Notice	When needed. Not necessary when an indicative notice has been published
Last date for receipt of requests to tender or negotiate	In general 5 weeks, and in any event not less than 22 days, from dispatch of notice or invitation to tender or negotiate
Last date for receipt of tenders	To be agreed between the utility and those invited to tender. In the absence of agreement, to be fixed by the utility and shall be at least 3 weeks and in any event not less than 10 days from the date of dispatch of the invitation to tender. (Account should be taken of the time required for examination of voluminous documentation or the need to inspect the site)

(With or without call for competition)

Further information	Must be supplied no later than 6 days before the final date for the receipt of tenders (provided requested in good time and accompanied by fee)

All procedures

Award notice   Not later than 2 months after
                                the award

Technical specifications

All of the Directives contain similar provisions with regard to the use of technical specifications. The requirement is to use European specifications and standards whenever possible, and in their absence there is a hierarchy of other standards that may be used, these being international, national, and finally company standards if no others exist. By *European specification* is meant a common technical specification, a national standard implementing a European standard, or a European technical approval. A *common technical specfication* means a technical specification drawn up in accordance with procedures recognised by Member States with a view to uniform application in all Member States. European technical approvals were not available at the time of writing.

There is a list of circumstances in which a departure from European standards is permissible. The list varies in minor detail from directive to directive, but basically there are five exceptions: where there are mandatory requirements under national law which are not incompatible with European law; where it is technically impossible to use European specifications; where there would be a conflict with specific Community obligations such as those set out in the legislation on IT and tele-communications standards (Council Directive 91/263/EEC (OJ L128 23.5.91 p1) and Council Decision 87/95/EEC (OJ L36 7.5.87 p31); and for innovative projects where European standards would be inappropriate.

Selection criteria

All of the Directives contain broadly similar lists of selection criteria. There are two lists.

The first is a list of criteria on the basis of which a supplier, contractor or service provider may be excluded from participation in the contract. The criteria listed under this head are (taking the Supplies Directive as our example): bankruptcy and insolvency; criminal offences or grave misconduct in the course of the business; failure to fulfil social security or tax obligations; serious misrepresentation in relation to the selection criteria; non-registration on a professional or trade register; failure to meet the economic and financial standing required by the contracting authority; or failure to meet standards of technical capacity.

The second is a list of the kind of information that an authority can ask for with regard to economic and technical standards. The authority may take account of statements of the supplier's bankers, or, for example, a statement of overall turnover, and the turnover of goods (of the type proposed to be supplied) in the three previous financial years. On the technical side it may take account of the supplier's technical facilities, measures for ensuring quality, study and research facilities and so on. The particular criteria are summarised for each regulation in Chapters 5–8.

Post tender negotiations

Negotiations on fundamental aspects of the contract, in particular prices, are ruled out in the period between tender and award. Discussion may be held only with the object of clarifying the bid, or the requirements of the contract authority, and provided this does not involve discrimination. This view is expressed in the Commission Statements on post-tender negotiation (OJ L111 30.4.94 p22, and OJ L210 21.7.89 p22). For an example of the sort of conduct that results in difficulty, see the *Wollonia Buses* case, C-87/94-R *Commission* v. *Kingdom of Belgium* [1994] ECR I-1395. What happened in this case was that Société Régionale Walonne du Transport (Walloon Regional Transport Company – SRWT), which is based in Namur, put out an invitation to tender for the supply of some 307 buses. SRWT examined the tenders and recommended that the first lot be awarded to Jonkheere and the second to Van Hool. A third company, EMI, then sent three memoranda to SRWT relating to discounts, replacement gearboxes, and fuel consumption rates. SRWT promptly changed its mind and awarded the second lot to EMI.

This was a failure to comply with the principle of equal treatment that underlies all the Directives, and an example of unfair post-tender negotiation. Van Hool therefore brought an action in the Belgian Conseil d'Etat for an order suspending the operation of the decision, but this was dismissed. The Commission therefore made an application to the European Court for the adoption of interim measures suspending the contract. The only reason the Commission lost this application was that by allowing 3 months between receiving the complaint and informing the Member State of its intention to seek suspension of the contract the Commission did not display the diligence expected of it. (A fuller account of this case is given in Chapter 9.)

Award criteria

A contract must be placed either on the basis of the offer that is the most economically advantageous to the authority or on the basis of the lowest price. The criteria used to determine economic advantage must appear in the contract notice, preferably in descending order, and the permitted criteria are listed in broadly similar terms in each of the Directives. To take the Supplies Directive as our example, they are set out in article 26 of the Directive, namely 'various criteria according to the contract in question: e.g. price, delivery date, running costs, cost-effectiveness, quality, aesthetic and functional characteristics, technical merit, after-sales service and technical assistance'. If a contracting authority fails to set out the award criteria in the contract notice it cannot rely on criteria of economic advantage, and may be driven to accept the lowest price: see *R* v. *Portsmouth City Council* ex parte *Coles, The Times*, 13 November 1966, *Commission* v. *Belgium* (C-87/94), ECJ unreported transcript, and *Gebroeders* v. *The Netherlands* (C31/87) [1988] ECR 4635.

Chapter 3

Practical Concerns

In this chapter we shall consider what burdens the Directives impose on purchasing authorities, the utilities, and their suppliers. There are four matters of concern: complication, dislocation, litigation, and administration. Complication because there are six directives, four sets of regulations, and a set of tedious procedures with time limits. Dislocation because suppliers can no longer depend upon the loyalty of their customers. Litigation, because suppliers can now seek orders for damages and other remedies from the High Court. Administration, because staff must be trained and allocated to the task of complying with the Directives.

Problems for the purchaser

The Directives are complicated, but there are compensating benefits. Because sanctions can now be imposed, purchasing authorities are more scrupulous in their adherence to the rules than was once the case. In those Member States where peculation is rife, there is a greater visibility of dealings. The Directives also impose better planning, improve administrative procedures, and direct negotiations towards the clarification of bids.

If the procedures are used as a means of reviewing an entire purchasing system, outdated practices can be eliminated. A case in point is the predilection of the public sector to decide on a particular requirement, and rush to take the lowest bid, only to find that the requirement has re-arisen. In a fuss, a whole process has to be done again. The Directives, by necessitating a planned approach, eliminate this kind of inefficiency, and encourage an annual consolidation of needs.

On the other hand, rigid planning puts the buyer at a disadvantage when he has to prequalify contractors from other Member States, or when the timescales imposed by the Directives are inconvenient. For example, a utility that fails to plan an advertisement for an outdoor activity may miss a period of clement weather, and lose a year on a project.

Small departments have a particular handicap when it comes to realising the benefits of complex procedures. The thresholds under the various Directives are set high in order to prevent them from becoming a burden, but supplies and works contracts for high-spending departments in central government, such as the Department of Social Security, the Ministry of Defence and the Home Office, can easily reach such levels. A small department in central government may find that it is rarely faced with a purchasing requirement, but when the event happens the task of complying with the Directives is a major exercise. In a small department there is no spare administrative capacity or expertise, because large purchases are made infrequently, but staff move every 2 or 3 years.

Where a local authority or development authority is operating a system of compulsory competitive tendering it has the added burden of applying the Directives, although in large measure the two regimes are compatible.

Philosophical differences

Differences in philosophy and practice between the United Kingdom, its partners in Europe, and the Commission also cause difficulties for buyers. In the UK, partnership (a concept that we shall consider below) is encouraged, and cooperative arrangements such as the Private Finance Initiative. The UK government prefers the negotiated procedure, and states in its White Paper *Setting New Standards, a Strategy for Government Procurement*, Cm 2840, that 'relationships with suppliers will combine competition with cooperation' (see paragraph 2.53), whereas the Commission would like to see open competition as the norm.

Another difference between between the United Kingdom and the rest of the European Union is that in most Member States there are official lists of public works contractors, whereas in the United Kingdom each authority keeps its own list, much like a private company. Companies from other Member States are likely to misinterpret this as discrimination against them.

Problems for the supplier

The supplier will not generally be concerned with the Directives; his only concern is to make his bid in accordance with the terms of the published notice. The supplier must be aware of the time limits, of the criteria for making awards, and of the available remedies if he is unfairly treated, but the complication is mainly for the purchaser.

Nevertheless, the supplier does not come off lightly, for the new regime dislocates long-term relationships, and is really suitable only for the purchase of commodities, and short-term contracts, not for developing long-term relationships. Before the present emphasis on competitive tendering there used to be a system, with British Telecom for example, of bulk supply agreements. Contractors were willing to put up with the short-term disadvantages of such arrangements in return for long-term stability. Under the new regime past loyalty is not an element of either the lowest price, or the most economically advantageous tender. Customer loyalty is difficult in the case of open tendering, less so in the case of the restricted procedure, and in the case of some government departments operating rotating bidders lists (suppliers ABC, then BCD, then CDE) practically impossible.

An effect of the dislocation of long-term relationships is that it is now impossible to leave the detail of a tender to post-tender negotiations. If the relationship with the supplier is more formal, and if the customer is not permitted to take the rough with the smooth, then the detail of the contract must be formulated at a much earlier stage. This means that the cost of preparing a tender has become a significant factor. It may cost many thousands of pounds to tender for a complicated engineering project, and many companies do not submit tenders because of the cost of presentation.

Some areas of commerce do not lend themselves to open tendering. In purchasing theory, open tendering is suitable only for off-the-shelf, identical, items – in other words for commodity items. For the purchase of a service an iterative process is best. In the case, for example, of a consultancy study, the competent buyer will first establish who is known to do such work, taking also a view of how large the organisation would have to be to cope with the work. The buyer would then invite expressions of interest and deliver outline requirements, hold a beauty parade, and then reduce the bidders to a shortlist. The full specification would be sent only to the small number of people thus known to be able to provide the service. If open tendering is used for an incomplete specification the buyer will not get what he wants, and comparison will be impossible. For this reason some contractors decline to bid because they know that the chances of success are small.

The European Union itself is notorious for its use of open procedures for its procurement, with the result that the Commission's quality assessment is often poor, and it tends to prefer academics to practitioners in the case of consultancies.

Litigation

Few cases have reached the courts in the United Kingdom, but this does not reflect the process on the Continent, where such actions are commonplace. Because contracts may be placed only by reference to set criteria, the fact of having complained in the past, or of having been loyal in the past, will have no effect on the choice of contractor. In consequence the supplier has less to lose in litigation. A contractor who is a supplier throughout Europe will also reflect that he is not limited to the courts of the United Kingdom; if he has been refused a contract in a foreign jurisdiction he may wish to sue there. In Europe the courts do not, as a rule, award costs; each side bears his own costs, and the costs of lawyers in other jurisdictions are lower than in the Common Law jurisdictions. In consequence we must expect that there will be an increase in litigation in the area of public procurement.

Partnership sourcing

Competition is not always good. The story of the United Kingdom electronics industry is a case in point. There was a strong consumer electronics industry in the years immediately after the Second World War. The makers of televisions established a tradition of bargaining with component suppliers for the lowest possible price, and dropping them without hesitation in favour of a competitor who offered a cheaper product, or who overcame technical difficulties. This policy drove out of business the suppliers who produced the best quality components, and encouraged those who provided the cheapest. The Japanese adopted a stable relationship with their suppliers, supporting them when necessary and helping them to remain competitive. They were therefore able to produce televisions that were more reliable than those of their competitors, and decimated the UK manufacturers.

Competitive tendering is a good policy for a company when there is no doubt about the firm's needs and there are several reliable suppliers to choose from. But when the market is changing, or when its characteristics cannot be measured, it is difficult to specify those needs. In such uncertainty the buyer cannot rely upon the supplier if he treats him as a mere adversary. In the jargon used by academics, the buyer will prefer *partnership sourcing*. A partnership in this sense means the use of long-term contracts, reduced sources of supply, and a high degree of trust between the parties. It is a long-term relationship involving collaboration and mutual respect. It is difficult to see how such relationships can survive in the path of the Purchasing Directives.

In the White Paper *Setting New Standards: A Strategy for Government Procurement* (1995) the Government states that:

> Competition will remain the cornerstone of government procurement policy. It is important not only as an aid to the achievement of value for money, but also because it provides fair access to work paid for by tax payers.

This policy matches the philosophy behind the Purchasing Directives, but it is ill founded because success in capitalism demands commitment, and this can be achieved only by a fusion of cooperation and competition.

Information technology

It is doubtful that any benefit may be got in the way of increased trade between Member States by inflicting the Purchasing Directives upon the information technology industry. The business is already global, and dominated by international companies who have established themselves across the European Union. There are no truly national suppliers who could be chosen, even if the purchaser wished to do so.

Open tendering is an inadequate method for choosing an appropriate supplier in this field. The purchaser usually does not know enough about the system that he wishes to buy to be able to formulate a specification for the work. Once work has begun the specification may change. Computer systems develop so quickly that by the delivery date the computer that was specified will have become obsolete, so that the tender that matches the advertised specification will be the worst choice. As the work progresses, systems are developed that were never envisaged, and the process of development is one in which vendor and purchaser are jointly involved. If an independent consultant is employed to formulate the specification for the work this may help the purchaser, but the problem of the evolving specification will still remain.

The advertising requirements and the strict timetables of the Directives serve to compound the problems of public sector purchasing of information technology. It takes a long time to obtain a public funding agreement. The Public Expenditure Survey (PES) is set up months in advance, and bids from departments are not ratified until close to the beginning of the financial year, when each department then struggles to spend its capital budget within the year. (The UK is, however, moving towards committment accounting, from April 1998, which should allow long-term contracts to be digested.)

Some authorities have entered into contracts for the management of their information technology facilities. The facilities management company thus acquires the technology on behalf of the authority, and relieves the authority of the burden of acquiring technical expertise. But such arrangements do not relieve the authority of its obligations under the Directives.

Post-contract negotiations do not provide a way out of the purchaser's dilemma, because these may be entered upon only to clarify the bid: see the Commission statement on post-tender negotiations (OJ L111 30.4.94 p114).

As a criterion for making the award of a contract for the supply of information technology, the lowest price can never be appropriate: the most economically advantageous tender is likely to be the one that offers the lowest overall cost of use (or put another way, the one that offers the best value for money). A way of coping with technological change is to include a clause in the specification to the effect that the purchaser will reserve the right to substitute items offering improved price performance. Such a clause is known as a *technology exchange clause*, and it permits the purchaser to take variants, by way of technically improved hardware and upgraded software.

Framework agreements

A framework agreement, sometimes called a *call-off agreement* because the purchaser can call off items as the need arises, may also provide a more flexible basis for the provision of information technology. Framework agreements are not contracts, but may be treated as such for the purposes of the Directives, and are specifically provided for under the Utilities Directive: the UK negotiated for this at the time the Directive was proposed, because it reflects standard UK commercial practice - see article 1(4), which describes the purpose of such an agreement, namely 'to establish the terms, in particular with regard to prices and, where appropriate, the quantity envisaged, governing the contracts to be awarded during a given period'. Although not mentioned in the Supplies or Services Directives, such agreements are recognised by the Commission.

Framework agreements are particularly useful for pan-government agreements, such as those negotiated by the CCTA, the Buying Agency. They enable small departments to take advantage of the government's overall buying power. The problem with this kind of agreement is, however, that the amount of further business cannot always be assessed. The advertising requirements in the Directives require the maximum spend to be publicised. The original advertisement may thus become obsolete, but cannot be extended.

Qualification systems

The Utilities Directive permits the utilities to operate vendor qualification systems, under article 30. The system 'may involve different qualification stages, shall operate on the basis of objective criteria and rules to be established by the contracting entity'. In accordance with this requirement the utilities have to circulate questionnaires. The response to these has never been good, perhaps because suppliers have yet to realise that purchasers have no option but to operate the systems required by the Directives, or perhaps because they do not appreciate that the bureaucratic effort is worthwhile. A failure to provide information ensures that a supplier will not be able to tender or negotiate for contracts.

Notices

Article 25 of the Utilities Directive states that contracting entities must be able to provide proof of the dispatch of notices. The cost of publication is borne by the Communities (at least something is free), and the notices are supposed to be published in full in their original language, together with a summary in the other official languages, and in the Tenders Electronic Daily (TED) database. The Office for Official Publications of the European Communities is obliged to publish the notice 'not later than 12 days after dispatch'. In exceptional cases it 'shall endeavour to publish the notice ... within five days'. In fact the publication is often delayed, sometimes by months. Because the time limit for the receipt of tenders in, for example, the open procedure is fixed at not less than 52 days from the date of dispatch of the notice, this presents a difficulty in complying with the timetable. The number of notices that the *Official Journal* has to deal with, bearing in mind the expansion not only of the Community but also of the scope of the Directives, has meant that the *Official Journal* does not translate the notices. An attempt is being made to enable computers to mechanically translate notices, by introducing a system of product coding, the Community Procurement Vocabulary (CPV), based on an earlier Code of Products by Activity (CPA). The Commission has also introduced a scheme for the use of data entry points, at which notices can be directly keyed onto a database.

The end result of this tinkering is that the notices produced in the *Official Journal* are comprehensible neither to man nor machine, and we must wait until this problem is overcome before the system of publication of notices can achieve its purpose.

Many notices are defective. A research project by the University of Ulster (see Ruth Hagan (1996) *Training for Quality*, IPSERA, Eindhoven) has shown that the most common omission in contract notices is that the award criteria are missing. Contract award notices frequently do not contain the prescribed information. Of 167 award notices published in 1995, 30 contained errors, the most frequent being the omission of the date of the original invitation to tender. Moreover, in 1994 time limits for the invitation to tender or contract award notice were not followed in 21 out of 291 cases. This research was limited to Northern Ireland, but it is sufficient to show that the Purchasing Directives are too complicated to achieve their objectives.

Private Finance Initiative

The Private Finance Initiative is a scheme introduced by the UK government with the object of obtaining private finance for public sector projects. To take a simple example, a contractor is invited to build a motorway in return for the right to the tolls. The Channel Tunnel Rail Link will be financed in this way, but with a far more complicated risk-sharing formula. Schemes have also been developed in the NHS and prison service, and it is intended to extend the system to the furthest reaches of public sector purchasing.

Problems arise with PFI contracts because the expense of tendering for PFI contracts, and the prolixity of the negotiations, make the open and restricted tendering processes highly unsuitable. Works concession contracts are subject to a modified regime. A *works concession contract* is defined in the Works Directive as a contract where the consideration consists 'either solely of the right to exploit the construction or in this right together with payment'. It is necessary to place a contract notice in the *Official Journal* in the case of a works concession contract (see article 3 of the Works Directive and regulation 25 of the Works Regulations). Moreover, the company that enters into a PFI project may find that it is itself subject to the Works Directive. Under article 3, Member States must ensure that a concessionnaire (other than a contracting authority) must apply the advertising rules to contracts that it awards to third parties (this is implemented by regulation 26). In the case of subsidised works contracts, that is to say certain contracts (including, apparently, concession contracts) that a purchasing authority subsidises by more than 50%, the subsidised body must comply with the Works Regulations as if it were a contracting authority (see regulation 23, implementing article 3). Subsidised public services contracts connected with these kinds of contract are subject to similar rules (see article 3 of the Services Directive and regulation 25 of the Services Regulations).

In the case of services concession contracts the position is less clear. According to the Services Regulations a public services contract does not include a case where the contracting authority engages a person to provide services to the public lying within its responsibility and under which the consideration given consists of or includes the right to exploit the provision of the services (see the definition of a public services contract in regulation 2). This exemption does not appear in the Directive. It may not have been what the Council intended, but the words of the Directive do not exclude the possibility that the concession contracts come within the full regime of the Directive.

The UK government has suggested that the negotiated procedure can be used in PFI schemes, but this could seldom be justified on the basis of any of the exclusions listed in the Directives, though it might sometimes be argued that overall pricing is impossible.

Chapter 4

Compulsory Competitive Tendering

In this chapter we shall consider the nature of the law on compulsory competitive tendering (CCT). Purchases by local authorities, and certain other defined authorities, are affected, and therefore the buyer needs to know whether he must operate the EU purchasing regime, or CCT, or both, and he must consider whether there are any conflicts between the two systems. The vendor of goods and services, and works contractors, must know whether the regulation of their transactions stems from CCT, from the EU regime, or from both.

The purpose of CCT

The object of the rules governing compulsory competitive tendering is different from that of the Public Procurement Directives. The rules on compulsory competitive tendering are designed to control direct labour organisations (DLOs) and direct service organisations (DSOs) by opening up the purchasing procedures of local authorities to commercial pressures. In broad terms, the CCT legislation prevents a DLO or DSO from undertaking any work unless it has made a bid for the contract in competition with private sector contractors. The Public Procurement Directives are designed for the very different task of creating conditions conducive to fair competition between Member States of the European Union. A local authority must comply with both regimes, but they do not, as a rule, overlap. Should there be a conflict the law of the European Union prevails (see 106/77 *Simmenthal* [1978] ECR 629 and C-6&9/90 *Frankovich v Republic of Italy* [1993] 2 CMLR 66, [1991] ECR I-5357). Nevertheless, the parallel operation of the two regimes does cause practical difficulties, and the vocabulary leads to confusion. In the CCT legislation reference is made to 'works contracts', but this does not refer to that term as it is used in the Works Directive, where the reference is to the activities listed in Annex II of professional activities as set out in the General Industrial Classification of Economic Activities within the European Communities. Thus a 'works contract' under the CCT may include work of a kind covered by the Services Directive. As to supply contracts, part II of the Local Government Act 1988 prevents public authorities from having regard to non-commercial matters in their purchasing policies, but supply contracts are not otherwise affected by CCT, because CCT is concerned not with the purchase of supplies but with the work done by local and development authorities through their direct labour organisations.

The system of compulsory competitive tendering was first introduced by the Local Government Planning and Land Act 1980. The 1980 Act is limited to works of construction and maintenance, and is aimed at the control of direct labour organisations in local government. The Local Government Act 1988 extended CCT to *defined authorities* (mainly local authorities and development authorities) and to a list of *defined activities*. This list, which the Secretary of State has power to extend, consisted of mainly manual activities. The Local Government Act 1992 makes amendments to both the earlier Acts. It implements the Citizens Charter (Cm 1599/1991) and the White Paper *Competing for Quality* (Cm 1730/1991), with the objective of making local authorities more accountable. The 1992 Act extends CCT to white collar work, broadens the power of the Secretary of State to add to the list of defined activities contained in the 1988 Act, and enables him to make regulations defining competitive and anti-competitive behaviour for the purposes of the Acts.

We shall consider in turn the detail of the Local Government Acts of 1980, 1988 and 1992 in order to see how the system has developed.

The Local Government Planning and Land Act 1980

Part III of the Local Government Planning and Land Act 1980 contains the earliest legislation on CCT. It controls the power of authorities to carry out construction and maintenance work for other bodies, and obliges authorities to invite tenders, keep separate accounts for DLOs, and publish reports on the works contracts they undertake.

By virtue of section 7 of the Act, a local authority may not enter into a works contract under which it is to carry out work whose value exceeds a prescribed amount unless it does so as the result of the acceptance of a tender, nor may it enter into a works contract under which it is to carry out work whose value is equal to or less than the prescribed amount unless it has complied with such conditions as may be prescribed by the Secretary of State. A *works contract* in this section means *inter alia* an agreement that provides for the carrying out by a local authority of any construction or maintenance work. The regulations made under section 7 are the Local Government (Direct Labour Organisations) (Competition) Regulations 1989 (SI 1989/1588) as amended by the Local Government (Direct Labour Organisations) (Competition) (Amendment) (England) Regulations 1994 (SI 1994/1439). The effect of these regulations is to make the distinction between contracts above and those below the prescribed amount irrelevant, so that no works contract may be entered upon unless by reason of the acceptance of a competitive tender, save for cases of urgency. There used to be an exemption from the tendering requirement in the case of gritting and clearing snow from highways, and also in respect of a percentage of general highway work, but the above regulations have repealed both exemptions.

For the purposes of the Act an authority enters into a contract as the result of the acceptance of a tender if the contract was made by acceptance of an offer on its part to carry out the work, and it made the offer in response to an invitation to submit such offers, and the invitation was extended to at least three other persons who are not, or include at least three persons who are not, local authorities or development bodies. Subsection 1A of section 7 of the Act was inserted by the Local Government Act 1988. It introduced what is known as the *competition condition*, namely that a local authority may not enter into a works contract under which it is to carry out work unless the other party to the contract in entering into it, and doing anything else in connection with it before entering into it, did not act in a manner having the effect or intended or likely to have the effect of restricting, distorting or preventing competition. The Local Government (Direct Service Organisations) (Competition) Regulations 1993 (SI 1993/848) as amended by the Local Government (etc) Amendment Regulations 1995 (SI 1995/1336), made under the Local Government Planning and Land Act 1980, the Local Government Act 1988, and the Local Government Act 1992, seek to prescribe and describe what amounts to anti-competitive behaviour. Regulations 4 and 5 prescribe with respect to steps in the tendering procedure, including the preparation and evaluation of an authority's own bid and announcing who should carry out the work, conduct which is to be regarded as having the effect, or likely effect, of restricting, preventing or distorting competition. Such conduct includes, for example, giving to a direct service organisation information about the work in addition to the information contained in the tender documents without giving the same information to each of the contractors; or announcing who is to undertake or carry out work later than 90 days after the expiry of the period within which contractors are allowed to respond to the invitation to tender for the work. Under regulation 15(1) of the Regulations the Secretary of State must issue guidance as to how conduct restricting, distorting or preventing competition is to be avoided. This guidance, the latest being DOE Circular 5/96, has to be taken into account in determining whether any competition condition has been fulfilled. This attention to detail contrasts with the Directives, which contain no detailed description of anti-competitive behaviour.

The Local Government Act 1988

Part I of the Local Government Act 1988 extended the scope of compulsory competitive tendering from mere works contracts to a list of defined activities (see section 2 and Schedule 1 of theAct) carried out by certain defined authorities (see section 1). The list covers not only manual work such as the collection of refuse and the cleaning of buildings, but also management of vehicles, housing management and legal services; the latter were added by the Local Government Act 1988 (Competition) (Defined

Activities) Order 1994 (SI 1994/2884). The Secretary of State may by order add other activities; the power to add professional services to the list was acquired by virtue of section 8 of the Local Government Act 1992, which permits him not only to add to the list in the 1988 Act (a power that he already possessed) but also to modify the Act where it is expedient for that purpose. Under the 1992 Act, CCT may be extended to work that consists in, or involves the provision of, professional advice or of other professional services, or the application of any financial or technical expertise. The Secretary of State may also exempt some defined activities carried out by defined authorities. For example, the Local Government (Defined Activities) (Exemption) (England) Order 1989 (SI 1989/2243) exempts the cleaning by the Common Council of the City of London of the Central Criminal Court. Generally exemption is granted where the annual expenditure on that activity in the previous year did not exceed £100,000.

The key section of the Local Government Act 1988 is section 4, which states that if a defined authority (a bidding authority) proposes to enter into a works contract (which means a contract constituting or including an agreement that provides for the carrying out of work by a defined authority) with another person, and under the contract the bidding authority is to carry out work falling within a defined activity, the bidding authority may not enter into the contract unless two precedent conditions are fulfilled. The first condition has two alternatives: either the contract was made by acceptance of the bidding authority's offer, made in response to an invitation by the other party to submit such offers, and the invitation was made to at least three other persons, who are not defined authorities or include at least three persons who are not defined authorities; or the other party published, in at least one newspaper circulating in the locality and at least one circulating among persons who carry out work of the kind concerned, a notice inviting persons to submit offers to carry out the work. (Compare this with the advertising requirements in for example the Supplies Directive: see page 137.) The second condition is a competition requirement, namely that the other party, in entering into the contract and in doing anything else in connection with the contract before entering into it, did not act in a manner having the effect or intended or likely to have the effect of restricting, distorting or preventing competition; the offending behaviour is itemised in regulations 4 and 5 of the Local Government (Direct Service Organisations) (Competition) Regulations 1993 (SI 1993/848), and in the guidance issued under regulation 15(1) of the Regulations.

Part I of the Local Government Act 1988 also contains restrictions on when a defined authority may carry out *functional work*, that is, work carried out by a defined authority other than under a works contract, and work that is carried out otherwise than by a defined authority but which, because it is dependent upon, or incidental or preparatory to, other work that is functional, is treated as functional work done by the defined authority. Most of the work done by DLOs is functional work, being work that the authority does for itself. There are six conditions, set out in section 7 of the Act, with which the defined authority must comply before it can undertake this kind of work.

The conditions

The first condition is that, before carrying out the work, the authority must have published in at least one newspaper circulating in the locality in which the work is to be carried out and at least one publication circulating among persons who carry out work of the kind concerned, a notice containing specified information about the contract. Broadly this is analogous to the notice that must be sent to the *Official Journal* under the Directives, and the procedure that follows is effectively a restricted procedure. Regulation 2 of the Local Government (Direct Service Organisations) (Competition) Regulations 1993 (SI 1993/848) applies where neither the Public Works Directive nor the Public Services Directive applies. Regulation 2(2) states that the period that must elapse during which a contractor may give notice of a wish to carry out the work shall be a period of not less than 37 days from the date on which the notice is published. Regulation 2(3) states that the invitation to tender shall specify as the period within which contractors are allowed to respond to the invitation a period of not less than 40 days commencing on the date of the invitation. These periods are similar to those set by the Directives.

The second condition set out in section 7 of the Act is that the periods, place, time and charge (for purchase of the detailed specification) specified in the notice are reasonable; that before carrying out the work the authority made a detailed specification of the work available for inspection, and copies of it available for supply, in accordance with the notice; and that the detailed specification includes a statement of the period during which the work is to be carried out. None of these provisions is met by an analogous provision in the Directives, but there are related requirements, such as article 13 of the Works Directive, and articles 19 and 20 of the Services Directive, which require contract documents and supporting documents to be sent to the contractor within six days of receiving the application, and additional information to be supplied not later than six days before the final date for receipt of tenders.

The third condition is that the invitation to tender must have been made by the authority before carrying out the work, and not less than 3 nor more than 6 months after publishing the contract notice; that if more than three persons who were not defined authorities notified the authority, at least three of them were invited; that if less than four who were not defined authorities notified the authority, each of them was invited; and that, if a defined authority, or authorities, notified the authority, such one or more of them as the authority decided was invited to tender.

The fourth condition is that before carrying out the work the authority, through its direct labour organisation or similar, prepared a written bid. This bid must comply with rules, set out in section 8(3), which require the authority to account for the work on a basis of assumptions calculated to treat the direct labour organisation as if it were an independent contractor.

The fifth condition is a competition requirement, for which purposes it is necessary to look at regulations 4 and 5 of the Local Government (Direct Service Organisations) (Competition) Regulations 1993 (SI 1993/848); see above, page 74.

The sixth condition stipulates that in carrying out the work the authority must comply with the detail of the specification set out in the contract notice.

Section 8 of the Act contains certain refinements to the above conditions, even to the point of permitting the Secretary of State to provide by regulations that the contract period during which functional work is to be done shall fall within maximum and minimum time limits set by the minister: see, for example, the Local Government Act 1988 (Defined Activities) (Specified Periods) (England) Regulations 1988, SI 1988/1373 as amended.

Sanctions

Unlike the Directives, the CCT legislation does not provide any means by which aggrieved contractors may sue the authority (although it is open to them to use the ordinary principles of judicial review for the purpose of compelling an authority to act in accordance with the law). The Secretary of State is, however, entitled to make use of sanctions provided in sections 13 and 14 of the Local Government Act 1988. Under section 13, if it appears to the Secretary of State that in any financial year a defined authority has entered into a contract in contravention of the restrictions on works contracts in section 4, or of functional contracts in section 6, or of other parts of the Act, he may serve a notice on the authority requiring it to submit a written response in which it must either deny contravening the rules and justify that stance, or admit its fault and give reasons why the Secretary of State should not give directions under section 14 of the Act. Under section 14 the Secretary of State may direct, for example, that as from a given date the authority shall cease to have authority to carry out any work falling within the appropriate activity.

Non-commercial considerations

Part II of the Local Government Act 1988 contains provisions that prevent public authorities (as listed in schedule 2 of the Act) from taking into account non-commercial matters for the purpose of awarding public supply or works contracts; the contracts covered are those for the supply of goods or materials, for the supply of services or for the execution of works, and they therefore include all contracts within the regime of the Purchasing Directives.

Section 17 states that in relation to various functions connected with these contracts a public authority may not take account of non-commercial matters. Terms and conditions of employment by contractors of their workers or the composition of, the arrangements for the promotion, transfer or training of or the other opportunities afforded to, their workforces, whether their subcontracts with individuals constitute contracts for the provision as self-employed persons of services only, the conduct of contractors or workers in industrial disputes, the political affiliation of contractors, and so on, are regarded as non-commercial matters for the purposes of section 17. Such matters may not be taken into account in compiling approved lists of contractors, in selecting contractors from whom tenders are to be invited, in accepting tenders or the persons with whom to enter into a contract, or in the giving or withholding approval for, or the selecting or nominating of, persons to be subcontractors.

Section 18 of the Act relates to race relations matters, and appears to be the only mention of this subject anywhere in any of the EU and UK legislation considered in this book. The effect of this section is that, subject to certain exceptions, section 71 of the Race Relations Act 1976, under which local authorities are to have regard to the need to eliminate unlawful racial discrimination and promote equal opportunity, does not require or authorise a local authority to exercise its purchasing functions by reference to non-commercial matters. The exceptions are that a local authority may ask questions (as approved by the Secretary of State) seeking information or undertakings, or include in a draft contract or tender terms relating to workforce matters, and they may consider the responses, if any of these matters are reasonably necessary to secure compliance with section 71 of the 1976 Act.

The Local Government Act 1992

The Local Government Act 1992 makes changes to the CCT regime, but does not affect the basic structure. Part I of the Act implements proposals in the Citizens Charter (Cm 1599, 1991) and *Competing for Quality* (Cm 1730,1991) that are intended to make local authorities more accountable. Section 8 empowers the Secretary of State to extend CCT to professional and technical services. Section 9, as we have seen, enables the minister to make detailed regulations describing the nature of conduct that is to be regarded as restricting, preventing or distorting competition, or which is not regarded as having that effect.

Chapter 5

Public Supply Contracts

The purchasing of supplies in the public sector is governed by Council Directive 93/36/EEC coordinating procedures for the award of public supply contracts (OJ No L199 9.8.93 p1), commonly known as the *Supplies Directive*. This consolidating directive repeals Council Directive 77/62 (OJ L13 15.1.77 p1) as amended by Council Directives 80/767/EEC (OJ L215 18.8.80 p1) and 88/295/EEC (OJ L127 20.5.88 p1), and makes some changes to conform with the Public Services and Works Directives. Although the Supplies Directive should have been adopted by 14 June 1994, it was not properly implemented in the United Kingdom until the Public Supply Contracts Regulations 1995 (SI 1995/201) came into force on 21 February 1995; these regulations also implement the Compliance Directive, Council Directive 89/665/EEC (OJ L395 30.12.89 p33).

Application

The Regulations apply (see regulation 5) whenever a contracting authority seeks offers in relation to a proposed public supply contract, other than a public supply contract excluded from the application of the Regulations by virtue of regulations 6 or 7.

In the Directive *contracting authorities* are defined as the State, regional or local authorities, bodies governed by public law, and associations formed by one or several of such authorities or bodies governed by public law. There is a definition of 'a body governed by public law' in the Directive, but for States where the concept is unknown the Directive refers to a list of bodies and categories of bodies that fulfil the necessary criteria, which is set out in Annex I of Works Directive 93/37/EEC. The easiest way to understand the definition as it applies in the United Kingdom is to refer to regulation 3 of the Regulations. This contains the list of bodies taken from the Works Directive, but with the addition of a category of GATT (now replaced by the World Trade Organisation Government Puchasing Agreement – GPA) contracting authorities. Most government departments and organisations are included. Associations formed by one or more such bodies, such as joint ventures between two or more contracting authorities and companies formed by a contracting authority, would come within the definition. The GATT (GPA) authorities are listed in Schedule 1; at the time of writing they were mentioned only in the Supplies Regulations, but the GPA now extends to purchasing of supplies, services and works in both central and local government, and to some extent applies to utilities. Purchases within the scope of the GPA have legal effects outside the European Union. The entities affected are set out in annexes to the GPA agreement.

Regulation 3(1)(r) contains the broader category of a corporation or group appointed to act for the specific purpose of meeting needs in the general interest and not having an industrial or commercial character. This is derived from the definition of a body governed by public law to be found in the Directive: established for the specific purpose of meeting needs in the general interest, not having an industrial or commercial character, and having a legal personality, and financed for the most part by the State, or local authorities, or other bodies governed by public law, or subject to management supervision by those bodies, or having an administrative, managerial or supervisory board more than half of whose members are appointed by the State, regional or local authorities or other bodies governed by public law. What is important to this definition is State control or finance.

Definitions

It is not always easy to say which regulation applies to a particular contract. The Supplies Regulations do not define what is meant by a *supply*, but in article 1 of Council Directive 93/36/EEC *public supply contracts* are defined as contracts for pecuniary interest concluded in writing involving the purchase, lease, rental or hire purchase, with or without option to buy, of products between a supplier (a natural or legal person) and a contracting authority. The delivery of such products may include siting and installation. The supply of a bespoke software package would not appear to come within this definition, though it would fall within the scope of the Services Directive; the supply of standard software would, on the other hand, be a product and thus affected by the Supplies Directive. In the Regulations 'pecuniary interest' is translated as 'consideration (whatever the nature of the consideration)' and 'product' is translated as 'goods', a term that, as the Regulations make clear, includes electricity. It is indicated that where services are to be provided the contract will be a public supply contract only where the value of the consideration attributable to the goods and any siting or installation of the goods is equal to or greater than the value of the services. If the value of the services is greater than the value of the supplies then the Services Regulations apply. There is no provision to distinguish works contracts, but if the distinction is not obvious, reference should be made to schedule 1 of the Works Regulations, where there is a list of activities taken from the General Industrial Classification of Economic Activities within the European Communities (NACE); if the activity falls within this list it is a works contract.

A *supplier* means a person who sought, or who seeks, or who would have wished, to be the person to whom a public supply contract is awarded, and who is a national of and established in a Relevant State. Note that the origin of the goods is not relevant, only the nationality of the supplier. *Relevant State* means a Member State of the Union, and Hungary, Poland, Iceland, Norway, and Liechtenstein. Regulation 4 states that a contracting authority shall not treat a person who is not a national of and established in a Relevant State more favourably than one who is.

Exclusions

Regulation 6 sets out general exclusions from the Supplies Directive. The exclusions may be summarised as follows:

- secret and security contracts;

- defence contracts (within article 223(1)(b) of the EC Treaty);

- contracts where different award procedures apply (various international agreements for joint implementation of projects with non-relevant States, for stationing of troops, and award procedures of international organisations such as the UN);

- contracts governed by the Utilities Directive.

The final exclusion requires some explanation. A local authority or government department may, because it operates, for example, a bus service, be subject to the Utilities Directive. This is less of a problem in the case of the United Kingdom, where most utilities have been privatised. The Supplies Regulations do not apply where the contracting authority is seeking offers in relation to a proposed supplies contract for the purpose of carrying out an activity specified in the second column of Schedule 1 of the Utilities Regulations, other than an activity specified in paragraphs 2 and 3 of the Schedule: paragraph 2 refers to hydraulic engineering, irrigation or land drainage in cases where more than 20% of the total volume of water made available is intended for the supply of drinking water, and paragraph 3 refers to the disposal or treatment of sewage. Neither do the Supplies Regulations apply when a contracting authority exercises the activity in paragraph 1 of Schedule 1 of the Utilities Regulations (provision or operation of fixed networks providing a service to the public in connection with production, transport or distribution of drinking water) for the purpose of carrying out an activity specified in paragraphs 2 and 3.

Thresholds

Regulation 7 contains the provisions on thresholds. The Supplies Regulations do not apply if at the relevant time the estimated value of the contract (net of value added tax) is less than the relevant threshold. The relevant time (see regulation 7(11)) means the date on which a contract notice would be sent to the

Official Journal if the requirement to send such a notice applied to the contract: that is, as soon as possible after forming the intention to seek offers in relation to the contract. The *estimated value* for the purposes of the regulation is the value of the consideration that the contracting authority expects to give under the contract. If the contract is for the hire of goods for an indefinite or uncertain period then its value is taken over 4 years (48 × the monthly hire).

The level of the threshold depends upon whether the contracting authority is a central government GATT (now GPA) authority or not; to find out whether it is, look at Schedule 1 of the Regulations, where they are listed, and refer to the annexes to the GPA agreement. The GPA has introduced a complication in that, apart from the need generally to amend the Directives to bring them into line, the values in the GPA are expressed in Special Drawing Rights (SDR) whereas those in the Directives are in ECU. (A Special Drawing Right (SDR) is the international reserve unit of account developed by the International Monetary Fund.) The Commission should fix, every two years, the value in sterling of the various thresholds, and because the published sterling values are used there is no practical difficulty. At the time of writing no official notice has been published, nor have the Directives been amended. However, an informal notice was published at the beginning of 1996, and these values are set out in this book. At the time of writing the threshold for central government (GPA) authorities was 130,000 SDR fixed at the sterling equivalent of £108,667. For subcentral government authorities the threshold was £158,018 (200,000 ECU). In all cases the threshold for the indicative notice was £592,568 (750,000 ECU).

A table showing all the thresholds under the Supplies, Works, Services and Utilities Directives, and their corresponding value in sterling, may be found in Chapter 2.

Aggregation

The rules on thresholds are not to be circumvented by splitting a large contract into smaller contracts. Where a contracting authority has a single requirement for goods, and a number of public supply contracts has been, or is to be, entered into to fulfil that requirement, the estimated value of each contract is taken to be the aggregate of the value of the consideration that the contracting authority expects to give under each of the contracts (see regulation 7(4)). Where a contracting authority has a requirement over a period of time, and for that purpose enters into a series of contracts or a contract that under its terms is renewable, then the estimated value of a component contract is taken to be either the aggregate value of similar contracts over the previous 12 months (or financial year), or the estimated value of those expected to be placed in the next 12 months; see paragraph (6) of regulation 7(6) for the detail of how this system works. As much as an authority may not split up contracts, so it may not choose a valuation method in accordance with paragraph (6) in order to avoid the Regulations.

It is not necessary to aggregate the value of all contracts when the goods to be purchased or hired under the contract are required for the sole purposes of a discrete operational unit within the organisation of the contracting authority. Provided that the purchasing decision has devolved to that unit, and is taken independently of any other part of the contracting authority, the unit is treated separately, so that only the purchases of that unit need to be aggregated; see further, regulation 7(7).

Technical specifications

If a purchasing authority desires to lay down technical specifications for goods under a public supply contract, it must specify all of them in the contract documents, and as a rule must use European standards, if they exist. Regulation 8 of the Supplies Regulations deals with these requirements; regulation 8 of the Works Regulations, regulation 8 of the Services Regulations, and Regulation 11 of the Utilities Regulations are in substantially the same terms.

Normally, technical specifications must be defined by reference to any relevant European specifications. *European specification* means a common technical specification, a British standard implementing a European standard, or a European technical approval. A *common technical specification* means a technical specification drawn up in accordance with a procedure recognised by the Member States, with a view to uniform application in all member States, which has been published in the *Official Journal*. European technical approvals are not yet available: therefore the normal technical specification will be a British standard implementing a European standard, which is identified by its prefix (BS EN).

A list of the circumstances in which an authority may depart from European specifications is set out in paragraph (4) of regulation 8; they may be summarised as follows:

- *Mandatory requirements*
  Where the the authority is obliged to define the technical specifications by reference to technical requirements that are mandatory under United Kingdom law and not incompatible with EC law.

- *Impossibility*
  Where either the European specifications do not include provision for, or it is technically impossible to establish conformity to, relevant European specifications.

- *Incompatibility*
  It would oblige the authority to acquire goods incompatible with equipment already in use, or would entail disproportionate costs or technical difficulties.

- *Telecommunications, IT and other community obligations*
  Where use of European specifications would conflict with Council Directive 91/263/EEC (OJ L128 23.5.91 p1), Council Decision 87/95/EEC (OJ L36 7.2.87 p31) and other Community obligations relating to specific types of services, material or goods.

- *Innovation*
  The project is genuinely innovative, so that European standards would be inappropriate.

If a contracting authority proposes to rely on any of the above it must state in the contract notice which circumstance it relies on or, if that is impossible, it must specify the circumstance in the contract documents. In any event it must keep a record. If the Commission or a relevant State so require, this record must be sent to the Commission via the Treasury; it is a part of the machinery by which the Commission can operate the corrective mechanism of the Directive. Although a departure from European standards is allowed on the grounds of incompatibility with equipment in use, costs, or technical difficulties, the authority may do so only when it has a clearly defined and recorded strategy for changing over, within a fixed period, to European specifications.

There is a hierarchy to the specifications that may be used. First come any relevant European specifications, but in their absence the authority must use British technical specifications recognised as complying with the basic requirements specified in any Council Directives on technical harmonisation: in particular Council Directive 89/106/EEC which relates to standards and technical approvals for construction products. The authority may use British technical specifications relating to the design and method of calculation and execution of work or works and use of materials and goods. Technical specifications may also be defined by reference to British standards implementing international standards; other British standards and technical approvals; or any other standards.

In practice the process is as follows. The buyer must first consider whether there is a relevant European specification: that is, a United Kingdom standard implementing a European standard, a common technical specification, or a European technical approval. If a European specification exists it must be used unless one of the exceptions in regulation 8(4) applies (mandatory requirements, technical impossibility, conflict with IT standards directives, incompatibility, or innovation). If the exception is incompatibility there must be a recorded strategy to change to European standards.

In the absence of a European specification the following conditions apply. The buyer must define the technical specifications in the contract documents by reference to British technical specifications recognised as complying with the basic requirements specified in any Council directives on technical harmonisation, in particular Council Directive 89/106/EEC. The buyer may use British technical specifications relating to design and method of calculation of work or works and use of materials and goods. The buyer may use British standards implementing international standards, failing that other British standards and technical approvals, and failing that any other standards.

References to a specific make, source or process that have the effect of favouring or eliminating particular goods or suppliers, and references to trademarks patents and so on, are not permitted, unless the references are justified by the subject of the contract, or the goods cannot otherwise be intelligibly described, and provided that the references are accompanied by the words 'or equivalent'.

Prior information notices

Contracting authorities have to make their purchasing requirement known as soon as possible after the beginning of their budgetary year by means of an indicative notice showing the total procurement by product area that they intend to make during the subsequent 12 months. The product area is established by reference to the Classification of Products by Activity (CPA), which is determined by the Commission in consultation with Member States, established by Council Regulation 3696/93 (OJ L342 31.12.93 p1), and published from time to time in the *Official Journal*. The CPA nomenclature is to be replaced by the CPV, which is described in Chapter 2. The requirement is implemented by regulation 9, and the form of the notice is set out in Schedule 3 Part A of the Regulations. All contracting authorities must advertise, in the *Official Journal*, at the beginning of their financial year, certain supply contracts that they expect to award during the course of the year; prior to Council Directive 93/36/EEC only GATT authorities were required to do this.

The obligation to publish an indicative notice does not apply to contracts that are excluded from the Regulations by regulation 6 (general exclusions) or regulation 7 (contracts below the relevant threshold). There is also no obligation to publish an indicative notice if the total consideration under all the proposed contracts that are for the supply of goods falling within the same product area is expected to be less than 750,000 ECU. (The sterling equivalent of this figure was fixed at £592,568 from 1 January 1996, and is reviewed, usually every two years.)

Procedures

The procedures that must be used in relation to public supply contracts are set out in Part III of the Regulations. When seeking offers a contracting authority must use one of three procedures: the open procedure, whereby any person who is interested may submit a tender; the restricted procedure, whereby only those persons selected by the contracting authority may submit tenders; and the negotiated procedure, whereby the contracting authority negotiates the terms of the contract with one or more persons selected by it. There is a free choice in the use of the first two procedures, but the negotiated procedure may be used only in exceptional cases. Each of these procedures involves the publication of notices in the *Official Journal*, and there are stipulated minimum periods of time for suppliers to ask for information, make offers in response to notices, and so on. The forms of these notices are set out in Schedule 3 of the Regulations. Any notice required to be sent to the *Official Journal* must be sent by the most appropriate means to the Office of Official Publications of the European Communities (see further, Chapter 2).

The process of making an award involves three stages: the selection of the appropriate award procedure and publication of a notice; the selection of suppliers who can compete for the award; and the making of the award in accordance with the award criteria.

Selection of award procedures

Save when exceptional circumstances justify the use of the negotiated procedure, a purchasing authority must use either the open or restricted procedure (there is a free choice between the two) for the purpose of seeking offers in relation to a proposed public works contract; in practice, most contracts are placed by means of the restricted procedure. The circumstances in which the negotiated procedure may be used are set out in regulation 10, and may be summarised as when:

- the open or restricted procedure was discontinued
  - because of irregular tenders, or

- because the tenders have been excluded after evaluation under the open or restricted procedures;

● there were inappropriate or no tenders under the other procedures;

● the goods are manufactured solely for research, experimental or development work (but not if purchased to recoup costs etc.);

● for technical or artistic reasons, or when, because of exclusive rights, only particular persons can manufacture or supply the goods;

● because of urgency the time limits in the other procedures cannot be met;

● additional, or partial replacement, goods are required.

A number of ancillary conditions apply to the above exceptions. In the case of irregular, excluded or absent tenders the contract placed by negotiated procedure must be substantially the same as that which was proposed in the abortive open or restricted procedures (see regulation 10(3)). *Irregular tenders* includes tenders that fail to meet the contract specifications, offer impermissible variations, or fail to meet technical specifications. If the reason for the use of the negotiated procedure is that there are no tenders then a report must, if the Commission requests, be submitted to the Treasury for onward transmission to the Commission. The exception allowing for the use of the negotiated procedure when the goods are to be manufactured purely for the purpose of research, experiment, study or development does not apply when the goods are purchased to establish commercial viability, or to recover research and development costs. The negotiated procedure may be used in cases of extreme urgency, where the time limits under the Regulations cannot be met, but only where this is strictly necessary, and the urgency must be brought about by events unforeseeable by, and not attributable to, the contracting authority (see regulation 10(2)(e)).

The negotiated procedure is permitted when goods are required as a partial replacement for, or addition to, existing goods or an installation, but in this case it must be shown that recourse to another supplier would result in incompatibility with the existing goods, or disproportionate technical difficulties. The term of the contract, and of any other agreement entered into for the same purpose, should not be more than 3 years, unless there are reasons why this is unavoidable. It is important to recall that if the difficulties arise because of a departure from European standards, the authority may use non-European standards in contract documents only when it has a clearly defined and recorded strategy for changing over, within a fixed period, to European specifications (see regulation 8(5)).

The open procedure

As soon as possible after forming the intention to seek offers in relation to a public supply contract the authority must send a notice, in a form substantially corresponding to that set out in Part B of Schedule 3, to the *Official Journal*. The form contains prescribed information, including the name and address of the authority, form of contract, quantity of goods to be supplied and CPA (now CPV) reference number, final date for receipt of tenders, and main terms as to financing.

The final date for receipt of tenders must be not less than 52 days from the date of dispatch of the notice. Contract documents are to be sent within 6 days of receipt of a request from any supplier, provided that they are requested by the date in the contract notice, and that any fee specified in the notice accompanies the request. Further information reasonably requested by the supplier, provided that the request is received in sufficient time, must be supplied not later than 6 days before the final date for the receipt of tenders. If contract documents are too bulky to be supplied within 6 days, or it is necessary that suppliers be given the opportunity to inspect the premises at which the goods are to be used or documents relating to the contract documents (i.e. supporting documents), then the period of 52 days for receipt of tenders must be extended to allow for inspection.

The selection of candidates and the award of the contract must be made in accordance with the selection and award criteria set out in parts IV and V of the Regulations, as to which see below.

The restricted procedure

The restricted procedure is set out in regulation 12. As soon as possible after forming the intention to seek offers in relation to a public supply contract the authority must send a notice, in a form substantially corresponding to that set out in Part C of Schedule 3, to the *Official Journal*. The form contains prescribed information, broadly similar to that required for an open procedure notice, including the name and address of the authority, form of contract, quantity of goods to be supplied and CPA (now CPV) reference number, and final date for receipt of requests to participate.

The last date for receipt of requests to be selected to tender may not be less than 37 days from the date of dispatch of the notice. This period may be reduced to 15 days where 37 days would be impractical for reasons of urgency. The urgency is probably not something that the authority could rely on if it has brought about the situation itself.

The same selection criteria apply as in the case of the open procedure. That is to say, an authority may exclude a supplier from the selection of persons invited to tender if one of the criteria for rejection of suppliers in regulation 14 applies (these include bankruptcy, insolvency, and serious misprepresentation), or if he fails to satisfy the minimum standards of economic and financial standing and technical capacity required by the contracting authority: see page 94 below.

In making its selection and in issuing invitations to tender the contracting authority must not discriminate on the grounds of nationality of the Relevant State in which the tenderer is established. Provided that it is confirmed by letter dispatched before the last date for receipt of applications, an authority cannot refuse to consider an application to be invited to tender that is sent by telegram, telex, facsimile or telephone.

The number of persons invited to tender must be sufficient to ensure genuine competition. But the authority can limit its choice to a predetermined range, provided that the lowest number in the range is not less than 5 and the highest no more than 20; the range is determined in the light of the nature of the goods; and it is specified in the notice.

There is no time limit for the authority to chose its shortlist of candidates. It must send invitations to tender simultaneously to each of the suppliers selected to tender; each invitation must either be accompanied by the contract documents, or state the address for requesting them. Certain information must be included in the invitation to tender (see regulation 12(10)). This information is largely of a kind that in the open procedure is included in the notice at the outset, such as: the address to which requests for contract documents and further information relating to them should be sent, the final date for making such a request and the fee; the final date for receipt of tenders and address to which they are to be sent and the language in which they are to be drawn; a reference to the contract notice; an indication of the information to be included with the tender which may be required in connection with the supplier selection criteria; and the award criteria, if not specified in the contract notice.

The date that the authority must fix as the last date for receipt of tenders must be not less than 40 days from the dispatch of the invitation; this period must be extended if suppliers have to inspect premises at which the goods are to be used or inspect documents relating to the contract documents; and it may be curtailed to a period not less than 10 days if a longer period would be impractical for reasons of urgency (in which case the invitation must be sent by the most rapid means possible).

Further information relating to the contract documents, reasonably requested by a supplier, must be supplied not less than 6 days before the final date for receipt of tenders, but this period can be reduced to not less than 4 days where a longer period is impracticable for reasons of urgency.

The selection of candidates and the award of the contract must be made in accordance with the selection and award criteria set out in parts IV and V of the Regulations, as to which see below.

The negotiated procedure

The negotiated procedure is set out in regulation 13. The procedure takes two forms: with publication of a notice in the *Official Journal*, and without publication; in the latter case other formalities are dispensed with as well. The procedure without publication can be used when:

- the open or restricted procedure was discontinued, but only if the contracting authority invites to negotiate the contract every supplier who submitted a tender (not being an excluded tender) under the other procedures;

- there were inappropriate or no tenders under the other procedures;

- the goods are manufactured solely for research, experimental or development work (but not if purchased to recoup costs etc.);

- for technical or artistic reasons, or because of exclusive rights only particular persons can manufacture or supply the goods;

- because of urgency the time limits in the other procedures cannot be met;

- additional, or partial replacement, goods are required.

If publication of a notice is necessary the procedure is as follows. As soon as possible after forming the intention to seek offers the authority must send a notice in a form substantially corresponding to that set out in Part D of Schedule 3 inviting requests to be selected to negotiate. In the notice the last date for receipt of the requests must be specified, and it may not be less than 37 days from the date of dispatch of the notice. Where that minimum period is impracticable for reasons of urgency the authority may substitute a period of not less than 15 days, but in that event invitations to negotiate must be sent by the most rapid means possible. The authority is obliged to consider applications sent by letter – or by telegram, telex, facsimile or telephone if confirmed by a letter dispatched before the last date for receipt of applications. Where there is a sufficient number of persons who are suitable to be selected to negotiate, the number selected must not be less than three.

In any event, whether a notice must be published in the *Official Journal* or not, the selection of suppliers and criteria for excluding suppliers must be in accordance with the selection criteria as set out in regulations 14–17.

Selection criteria

In order to decide who shall be awarded a contract, an authority must apply certain award criteria (see regulation 21). But before the buyer can place a contract he must first consider the standing of the seller: that is, whether the contractor has the capacity to perform the contract, whether he is solvent, and whether he is trustworthy. The authority may exclude a supplier from consideration only if one of the criteria for rejection of suppliers in regulation 14 applies (these include bankruptcy, insolvency, and serious misprepresentation), or if he does not meet the standards of economic and financial standing or technical capacity set by the authority and assessed in accordance with regulations 15 and 16.

The factors that a contracting authority can take into account in measuring the standing of a contractor are referred to as the *selection criteria* or, to use the language of the Supplies Directive, the *criteria for qualitative selection*. In brief, these criteria are:

- Bankruptcy or insolvency

- a criminal offence relating to the conduct of, or an act of grave misconduct in the course of, the business or profession;

- failure to fulfil obligations relating to social security contributions or other taxes;

- serious misrepresentation in supplying information needed for the application of the selection criteria;

- whether the supplier is registered on a professional or trade register;

- failure to meet minimum standards of economic and financial standing set by the contracting authority;

- failure to meet minimum standards of technical capacity set by the contracting authority.

In most Relevant States there is an obligation to register on an appropriate trade register, such as the German Handelsregister or Handwerksrolle. In the common law countries there are no such registers: hence regulation 14(5) provides that a supplier established in the United Kingdom or Ireland shall be treated as registered on such a trade register if he is established in Ireland and certified as registered with the Registrar of Friendly Societies, or if he is established in either State and is either certified as registered with the Registrar of Friendly Societies, or is established in either State and is either certified as incorporated by the Registrar of Companies, or is certified as having declared on oath (in other words on affidavit) that he is carrying on business in the trade in question in the State in which he is established, at a specific place of business, and under a specific trading name. For an individual established in Spain there is a similar provision for a declaration on oath. And, for countries other than the United Kingdom and Ireland that have equivalent registers not listed in the regulations, or no registers, there is provision for the production of a certificate that the supplier is registered on an equivalent register, or for a declaration to be made on oath (see regulation 14(7)).

Information

Regulation 15 contains rules on the kind of information that the buyer can ask for when assessing whether a supplier meets any minimum standards of economic standing that he requires of suppliers. A contracting authority may take into account some or all of the following:

- statements from the supplier's bankers;

- statements of, or extracts from, accounts where publication is required by the law of the relevant state where the supplier is established (e.g. under the Companies Acts);

- a statement of overall turnover and the turnover in respect of goods (of a type similar to those proposed to be supplied), in the three previous financial years of the supplier.

Where this information is not appropriate the authority may require other information, but whatever is required must be specified in the contract notice or invitation to tender, and it may require no more than it needs to make the assessment or selection. A supplier who is unable, for a valid reason, to provide the information that the authority requires can provide other information, because the authority must accept such other information as it considers appropriate.

There is a limit on the information as to technical capacity that the authority may demand of a supplier. The categories of information are listed in regulation 16, which reproduces article 23 of the Directive, and concern the following:

- principal deliveries of similar goods over the past three years (when to a public authority, the evidence must take the form of a certificate from the authority, otherwise simply a declaration);

- the supplier's technical facilities, measures for ensuring quality, study and research facilities;

- the technicians or technical bodies involved, particularly those responsible for quality control; samples, descriptions and photographs, authenticity of which must be certified if the authority so requests;

- certificates of quality control agencies or institutes;

- where the products are complex or required for a special purpose, a check by the authority (or a competent official body on their behalf) of the production capacities and, if necessary, study and research facilities and quality control measures of the supplier.

Regulation 17 states that the authority may require supplementary information to be supplied under regulations 14–16, and regulation 18 states that it must comply with such requirements as to confidentiality as the supplier reasonably requests. The words of the Directive are stronger in this regard. Article 23(3) states that the information demanded on financial and economic standing and technical capacity must be confined to the subject of the contract, and the contracting authority must take into consideration the legitimate interests of the supplier as regards the protection of technical or trade secrets. Article 24 states that the contracting authority may invite suppliers to supplement the certificates and documents submitted or to clarify them; the Directive uses 'invite' but the regulation says 'require'.

Official lists

The official lists mentioned in regulation 19 have nothing to do with the kind of list that is drawn up as part of a prequalification system. In the Utilities Regulations there are rules about such lists, because all utilities operate a vendor qualification system to screen potential suppliers. The rules in the Supplies Regulations have to do with suppliers meeting formal minimum requirements. Where a supplier is registered on the official lists of recognised suppliers a certificate of registration must, in relation to most of the criteria for selection, be accepted as evidence that the supplier meets the necessary conditions, and the authority is not entitled to ask for supplementary information on matters covered by the certificate. Official lists do not operate in the United Kingdom.

Consortia

It is not necessary for the supplier to be a legal person in order to tender for a public contract. Regulation 20 therefore provides that a *consortium* means two or more persons, at least one of whom is a supplier, acting jointly for the purpose of being awarded a public supply contract. A contracting authority cannot refuse to consider a tender merely on the grounds that a supplier is a consortium. It can, however, require the consortium to form a legal entity before entering into, or as a term of, a contract.

A contracting authority may require a supplier to indicate in his tender what part of the contract he intends to subcontract to another person (see regulation 28).

The award criteria

A contracting authority must award its contract on one of two bases: either on the basis of the offer that is the most economically advantageous to the contracting authority, or on the basis of that which offers the lowest price. Where the basis of the award is to be the lowest price, the contract must go to the lowest tender; no other criteria can be considered, nor may variations be entertained.

When an authority intends to base the award on the most economically advantageous offer, the criteria must be stated, preferably in descending order, in the contract notice or contract documents. The criteria that it may use to determine that an offer is the most economically advantageous include delivery date, running costs, cost-effectiveness, quality, aesthetic and functional characteristics, technical merit, after-sales service, technical assistance and price. An authority can take account of an offer containing variations provided that the offer meets its minimum requirements, which it has stated, together with any specific requirements for making such an offer, in the contract documents. If it is not going to take notice of variations the authority must say so in the contract notice.

A contracting authority may not reject a variation on the grounds that it would lead to the award of a public services contract; this is a commonsense provision, which saves procedures from being gone twice over.

Contracting authorities may not reject a variant on the sole grounds that it has been drawn up with technical specifications defined by reference to national standards transposing European standards, to European technical approvals or to common technical specifications or by reference to national technical specifications of the kind mentioned in regulation 8(7)(a) and (b); the latter relate to specifications complying with basic harmonisation requirements or relating to design and methods of calculation and execution of work or works and use of materials and goods. This provision (see regulation 21(6)) permits the supplier who submits a variant to utilise standards that the buyer could have used in the contract documents; but the use of other standards, ISO for example, could be a sole ground for rejection.

Special rules apply to the rejection of an abnormally low offer; it may be rejected (even if price was the only basis of the award), but only if the authority has requested, in writing, an explanation. If price is the only basis of the award then the authority must examine the details of all the offers made and take into account any explanation given to it of the abnormally low tender; if economic advantage is the basis, then it must take into account any such explanation in assessing economic advantage. Explanations relating to economics of the manufacturing process, technical solutions suggested by the supplier, exceptionally favourable conditions, or the originality of the supplies may all be taken into account. But, if an offer is rejected as abnormally low, a report must be sent to the Treasury, for onward transmission to the Commission.

When one part of a contracting authority is invited by another to compete with outside offers, the rules permit the acceptance of in-house bids. An offer includes a bid by one part of a contracting authority to make goods available to another part.

Subcontractors

Regulation 28 states that a contracting authority may require a supplier to indicate, in his tender, what part of the contract he intends to subcontract to another person.

Award notices

An authority that has awarded a public supply contract must, no later than 48 days after the award, send to the *Official Journal* a notice substantially corresponding to the form set out in Part E of Schedule 3 making known the result. Information that might impede law enforcement or otherwise be contrary to public interest, prejudice commercial interests or fair competition need not be included.

Information about contract award procedures

Within 15 days of the date on which it receives a request from any unsuccessful supplier, the authority must inform the supplier of the reasons why he was unsuccessful, and the name of the person awarded the contract. The contracting authority has to keep a record in relation to each contract awarded of the main particulars of the award (as listed in regulation 23(2)). If the Commission so requests, a report containing this information must be sent to the Treasury for onward transmission to the Commission. Where an authority decides neither to award a contract nor to seek new offers, it must inform the *Official Journal* and (if asked) any suppliers who submitted offers, or who asked to participate in the tenders or negotiate for the contract.

Concessions

Part VI of the Regulations contains an important provision relating to service providers, namely that where a contracting authority grants a body special or exclusive rights to carry on a service for the benefit of the public it must impose an express duty on that person not to discriminate in awarding a supply contract on the grounds of nationality against nationals of a Relevant State on the grounds that the goods to be supplied originate in another Relevant State.

Statistics

Most of Part VI of the Regulations is concerned with provisions on the making of statistical reports. The background to this is article 31 of the Supplies Directive, which requires Member States to forward statistical information to the Commission in order to enable it to assess the results of applying the Directive. A GATT (now GPA central government) authority is obliged to send to the Treasury no later than 31 July each year a report specifying the aggregate value of the consideration paid for supply contracts below the threshold, and for each contract awarded above the threshold: the consideration, the procedure used (if negotiated, under which of the exceptions in regulation 10(2)), the type of goods and the nationality of the supplier to whom the contract was awarded. Other authorities have to send a similar report each alternate year, but it does not have to report on contracts below the threshold.

Chapter 6

The Works Directive

Council Directive 93/37/EEC of 14 June 1993 concerning the coordination of procedures for the award of public works contracts (OJ L199 9.8.93 p54) is a purely consolidating measure. It replaces Council Directive 71/305/EEC (OJ L185 16.8.71 p15) and its many amendments. The Works Directive is implemented in the United Kingdom by the Public Works Contracts Regulations 1991 (SI 1991/2680), which also implement the compliance directive, Council Directive 89/665/EEC (OJ L395 30.12.89 p33). The Regulations came into force on 21 December 1991, and have been amended, as from 13 January 1993, by regulation 32 of the Utilities Supply and Works Contracts Regulations (SI 1992/3279) for the purpose of correcting minor errors, and in order to make it clear that the Works Regulations do not apply to contracts in the utilities sector.

Application

The Regulations apply (see regulation 5) whenever a contracting authority seeks offers in relation to a proposed public works contract, other than one excluded by regulations 6 or 7.

For the most part the Regulations do not refer to concession contracts; these are defined in regulation 2 as 'a public works contract under which the consideration given by the contracting authority consists of or includes the right to exploit the work or works to be carried out under the contract', such as to build a road and thereafter manage it and take the tolls – a kind of contract not popular in the United Kingdom until the advent of the Private Finance Initiative. Regulations 25 and 26 contain particular rules about concession contracts, and these are discussed later in this chapter. In Parts II, III, IV and V of the Regulations and in regulations 24, 27 and 28 references to public works contract do not include public works concession contracts.

In the Directive *contracting authorities* are defined as the State, regional or local authorities, bodies governed by public law, and associations formed by one or several such authorities or bodies governed by public law. There is a definition in the Directive of a *body governed by public law*, but for Member States where the concept is unknown a list of bodies and categories of bodies that fulfil the necessary criteria is set out in Annex I of the Directive. The best way to understand the definition as it applies in the United Kingdom is to refer to regulation 3 of the Works Regulations, which contains a list of the relevant contracting authorities. Most government departments and organisations are included, local authorities, police, and fire authorities.

Regulation 3(1)(r) contains the broader category of a corporation or group appointed to act for the specific purpose of meeting needs in the general interest and not having an industrial or commercial character. This is derived from the definition of a body governed by public law to be found in the Directive: that is, established for the specific purpose of meeting needs in the general interest, not having an industrial or commercial character, having a legal personality, and financed for the most part by the State, or local authorities, or other bodies governed by public law, or subject to management supervision by those bodies, or having an administrative, managerial or supervisory board, more than half of whose members are appointed by the State, regional or local authorities or other bodies governed by public law. What is important to this definition is State control or finance.

Definitions

In the Regulations a *public works contract* means a contract in writing for consideration (whatever the nature of the consideration) for the carrying out of a work or works for a contracting authority, or under which a contracting authority engages a person to procure by any means the carrying out for the contracting authority of a work corresponding to specific requirements (see regulation 2). Design and build contracts are included in this definition because the description of 'public works contracts' in article 1 of the Directive includes contracts that have as their object either the execution, or both execution and design, of works. But contracts with mixed objectives may not always come within the definition. Thus, in Case C-331/92 *Gestión Hotelera Internacional SA* v. *Communidad Autónoma de Canarias* [1994] ECR I-1329, the question arose whether a mixed contract relating to the performance of works and the assignment of property was a works contract within the meaning of the Directive. The conditions of a tender relating to a publicly owned hotel business in the Canary Islands required the successful contractor to do renovation work to the hotel so that it could operate a casino. The European Court held that a contract for both the assignment of property and the doing of works did not fall within the Works Directive if the performance of the works was merely incidental to the assignment of the property.

There is a distinction between 'work' and 'works' for the purposes of the regulations, which it is important to understand because the aggregation rules depend upon it. *Work* means the outcome of any works that is sufficient in itself to fulfil an economic and technical function – the Directive says 'works taken as a whole' – and *works* means any of the activities specified in Schedule 1 of the Regulations, being activities contained in the general industrial classification of economic activities within the Communities. The French version of the Directive is clearer: 'On entend par *ouvrage* le résultat d'un ensemble de travaux de bâtiment ou de génie civil destiné à remplir par lui-même une fonction économique ou technique.' Schedule 1 contains a list of various building and engineering activities, such as the construction of buildings, broken down into individual tasks such as roofing or installation of electrical fittings. Thus, for example, installing wiring, or insulation, or roofing would be works, whereas the school thereby constructed would be a work. Subsequent repairs to the school would be works, but could not be said to be a work.

Sometimes there will be difficulty in determining whether a

contract is a works contract rather than a supply or service contract. Usually this can be resolved by an examination of the provisions of the parallel directive. Public service contracts, for example, in the field of property management may from time to time include some works, but where the works are incidental rather than the object of the contract they do not justify treating the contract as a public works contract.

Supply contracts, according to the definition in article 1 of the Supplies Directive, may include siting and installation: for example, a contract to supply double glazing. A problem of distinguishing such contracts from public works contracts can arise where goods are supplied for a construction project and the supplier is bound to incorporate them on the site. It is generally considered that if the value of the goods to be supplied exceeds that of the services to be performed, then it is a supply contract, but if the services are construction or civil engineering works of the type listed in Schedule 1 of the Regulations, and their value exceeds that of the goods, then it must be a public works contract. This accords with the definition of 'public supply contract' in regulation 2 of the Supplies Regulations, which includes siting or installation of the goods, but states that, where services are also provided, the contract is a public supply contract only where the value of the goods and installation is equal to or greater than the value of the services.

The overall intention of the Directives is that no contract, provided its value lies above one of the relevant thresholds, will escape the net; if it is not a works contract it will be a supplies, or services, contract. The only problem for the buyer is to determine which directive applies.

Exclusions

Regulation 6 sets out general exclusions from the Works Directive:

- secret and security contracts;

- contracts where different award procedures apply (various international agreements for joint implementation of projects with non-relevant States; for stationing of troops;

and award procedures of international organisations such as the UN);

- contracts governed by the Utilities Directive.

These exceptions do not differ in any material respect from those set out in regulation 6 of the Supplies Regulations (the reference to article 223 of the EC Treaty in the Supplies Regulations relates to contracts for the purchase of certain defence materials – this would hardly arise in a construction contract).

The Regulations do not apply where the contracting authority is seeking offers in relation to a proposed public works contract for the purpose of carrying out an activity specified in the second column of Schedule 1 of the Utilities Regulations, other than an activity specified in paragraphs 2 and 3 of the Schedule. Paragraph 2 refers to hydraulic engineering, irrigation or land drainage in cases where more than 20% of the total volume of water made available is intended for the supply of drinking water, and paragraph 3 refers to the disposal or treatment of sewage. Neither do the Works Regulations apply when a contracting authority exercises the activity in paragraph 1 of Schedule 1 of the Utilities Regulations (provision or operation of fixed networks providing a service to the public in connection with production, transport or distribution of drinking water) for the purpose of carrying out an activity specified in paragraphs 2 and 3.

Thresholds

The Regulations do not apply to the seeking of offers in relation to a proposed public works contract where the estimated value of the contract (net of value added tax) at the relevant time is less than 5,000,000 ECU (fixed in stirling at £3,950,456 for the period from 1 January 1996 and revised usually every two years). The *relevant time* (see regulation 7(7)) means the date on which a contract notice would be sent to the *Official Journal* if the requirement to send such a notice applied to the contract: in other words, as soon as possible after forming the intention to seek offers in relation to the contract. The *estimated value* is the value of the consideration that the authority expects to give under the contract. But in the case of a concession contract the value is taken to be the consideration that the authority would expect to give for carrying out the work if it did not propose to grant a concession. And where an authority intends to provide any goods for the purpose of carrying out a contract the value of the consideration is taken to include the value of the goods.

Aggregation

The rules on thresholds cannot be circumvented by splitting a large contract into small contracts. The usual rule is that the estimated value, for the purpose of calculating the threshold, of a contract that is one of a number of contracts entered into for the carrying out of a work is taken to be the aggregate of the value of the consideration that the contracting authority has paid, or expects to give, under all the contracts for carrying out of the work.

But the contracting authority may, if it chooses, make an exception and treat a contract as worth less than the threshold value if it is worth less than 1,000,000 ECU, and if the aggregate value of the contract, and any other contract in respect of which it chooses to take advantage of this exception, is worth less than 20% of the aggregate value of the consideration for the whole work.

What this means is that a number of small contracts, each worth less than 1,000,000 ECU, can be placed without using one of the award procedures, provided that the total value of the contracts treated in this way is not more than 20% of the value of the work taken as a whole. Thus, if a contract to build a school is split into five contracts, the first worth 2,000,000 ECU, the second worth 1,500,000 ECU, the third worth 750,000 ECU, and the fourth and fifth worth 625,000 ECU each, then the authority must use an award procedure in the case of the first and second contract, and it must use an award procedure for at least two of the remaining contracts; it may choose not to use the award procedure for one only of the last three contracts.

Technical specifications

If a contracting authority wishes to lay down technical specifications that the work or works and the materials and goods used must meet, it must specify them all in the contract documents, and as a rule must use European standards if they exist. Regulation 8 of the Works Regulations deals with these requirements; regulation 8 of the Supplies Regulations, regulation 8 of the Services Regulations, and Regulation 11 of the Utilities Regulations are in substantially identical terms. Normally, technical specifications must be defined by reference to any relevant European specifications. *European specification* means a common technical specification, a British standard implementing a European standard, or a European technical approval. A *common technical specification* means a technical specification drawn up in accordance with a procedure recognised by the Member States with a view to uniform application in all member States, which has been published in the *Official Journal*. European technical approvals are not yet available: therefore the normal technical specification will be a British standard implementing a European standard, identifiable by its prefix – BS EN.

A list of the circumstances in which an authority may depart from European specifications is set out in paragraph (4) of regulation 8. They may be summarised as follows:

- *Mandatory requirements*
  Where the the utility is obliged to define the technical specifications by reference to technical requirements that are mandatory under United Kingdom law and not incompatible with EC law.

- *Impossibility*
  Where either the European specifications do not include provision for, or it is technically impossible to establish conformity to, the European specifications.

- *Incompatibility*
  Where it would oblige the authority to acquire goods incompatible with equipment already in use, or would entail disproportionate costs or technical difficulties.

- *Innovation*
  Where the project is genuinely innovative, so that European standards would be inappropriate.

If a contracting authority proposes to rely on any of the above, it must state in the contract notice which circumstance it relies on, or if that is impossible it must specify the circumstance in the contract documents. In any event it must keep a record. If the Commission or a Relevant State so require, this record must be sent to the Commission via the Treasury; it is a part of the machinery by which the Commission can operate the corrective mechanism of the Directive. Although a departure from European standards is allowed on the grounds of incompatibility with equipment in use, costs, or technical difficulties, the authority may do so only when it has a clearly defined and recorded strategy for changing over, within a fixed period, to European specifications.

There is a hierarchy to the specifications that may be used. First come any relevant European specifications, but in their absence the authority must use British technical specifications recognised as complying with the basic requirements specified in any Council Directives on technical harmonisation – in particular Council Directive 89/106/EEC, which relates to standards and technical approvals for construction products. The authority may use British technical specifications relating to design and method of calculation and execution of work or works and use of materials and goods. Technical specifications may also be defined by reference to the following standards: British standards implementing international standards; other British standards and technical approvals; or any other standards. A *standard* means a technical specification approved by a recognised standardising body for repeated and continuous application, compliance with which is in principle not compulsory. ISO, DIN or ANSI standards or similar would be examples.

In practice the process is as follows. The authority must first consider whether there is a relevant European specification: that is, a United Kingdom standard implementing a European standard, a common technical specification, or a European technical approval. If a European specification exists it must be used unless one of the exceptions in regulation 8(4) applies (mandatory requirements, technical impossibility, incompatibility, or innovation). If the exception is incompatibility there must be a recorded strategy to change to European standards. In the absence of a European specification the following conditions apply. The authority must define the technical specifications in the contract documents by reference to British technical specifications recognised as complying with the basic requirements specified in any Council Directives on technical harmonisation, in particular Council Directive 89/106/EEC (OJ L140 11.2.89 p12). The authority may use British technical specifications relating to design and method of calculation of work or works and use of materials and goods. The authority may use British standards implementing international standards, or failing that other British standards and technical approvals, and failing that the buyer may use any other standards.

References to a specific make, source or process that have the effect of favouring or eliminating particular contractors, and references to trademarks, patents and so on, are not permitted, unless the references are justified by the subject of the contract, or the goods cannot otherwise be intelligibly described, and provided that the references are accompanied by the words 'or equivalent'.

Prior information notices

A contracting authority intending to seek offers in relation to a public works contract must, as soon as possible after the decision approving the planning of the work or works, send to the *Official Journal* a notice, in a form substantially corresponding to that set out in Part A of Schedule 2 of the Regulations. The notice contains *inter alia* information about the site, the nature and extent of the services to be provided, the date when the award procedures will begin, the date of start of the work and the timetable for completion.

Procedures

The procedures that must be used in relation to public works contracts are set out in Part III of the Regulations. When seeking offers, a purchasing authority must use one of three procedures: the open procedure, whereby any person who is interested may submit a tender; the restricted procedure, whereby only those persons selected by the contracting authority may submit tenders; and the negotiated procedure, whereby the contracting authority negotiates the terms of the contract with one or more persons selected by it. Each of these procedures involves the publication of notices in the *Official Journal*, and there are stipulated minimum periods of time for suppliers to ask for information, make offers in response to notices, and so on. The forms of notices are set out in the Schedule 2 of the Regulations. Any notice required to be sent to the *Official Journal* must be sent by the most appropriate means to the Office for Official Publications of the European Communities (see Chapter 2).

The process of making an award involves three stages: the selection of the appropriate award procedure and publication of a notice; the selection of contractors who can compete for the award; and the making of the award in accordance with the award criteria.

Selection of award procedures

Save where exceptional circumstances justify the use of the negotiated procedure, a purchasing authority must use either the open or restricted procedure (there is a free choice between the two) for the purpose of seeking offers in relation to a proposed public works contract. In practice, most contracts are placed by means of the restricted procedure. The circumstances in which the negotiated procedure may be used are set out in regulation 10, and may be summarised as when:

- the open or restricted procedure was discontinued
  - because of irregular tenders, or
  - because the tenders have been excluded after they have been evaluated under the open or restricted procedures;

- the contract is for research, experimental or development works (but not where the works are carried out in order to establish commercial viability or to recoup research and development costs);

- prior overall pricing is impossible;

- there were inappropriate or no tenders under the other procedures;

- for technical or artistic reasons, or because of exclusive rights, only particular persons can carry out the work;

- because of urgency the time limits in the other procedures cannot be met;

- additional works are necessary (but no more than 50% of the main contract);

- repetition works must be done (within 3 years).

A number of conditions apply to the above exceptions. In the case of irregular, excluded or absent tenders the contract placed by negotiated procedure must be substantially the same as that which was proposed in the abortive open or restricted procedures (see regulation 10(3)). *Irregular tenders* includes tenders that fail to meet the contract specifications, offer impermissible variations, or fail to meet technical specifications. If the reason for the use of the negotiated procedure is that there are no tenders then a report must, if the Commission requests it, be submitted to the Treasury for onward transmission to the Commission.

The negotiated procedure may be used in cases of extreme urgency, where the time limits under the Regulations cannot be met, but only where this is strictly necessary. The example usually given of this is the urgent repair of a dyke, but the urgency must be brought about by events unforeseeable by, and not attributable to, the contracting authority.

When a contracting authority wants the contractor to carry out additional works, the need must arise through unforeseen circumstances. There must be technical or economic reasons why the additional work cannot be carried out separately from the works under the original contract. If they can be done separately, however, the negotiated procedure can be used if the works are strictly necessary to the later stages of the contract. However, the value of contracts for additional work must not in aggregate exceed 50% of the value of the the original contract.

The open procedure

As soon as possible after forming the intention to seek offers in relation to a public supply contract the authority must send a notice, in a form substantially corresponding to that set out in Part B of Schedule 2, to the *Official Journal*. The form contains prescribed information, including the name and address of the authority, nature of contract, nature and extent of the services to be provided and general nature of the work, final date for receipt of tenders, and main terms as to financing.

The final date for receipt of tenders should be not less than 52 days from the date of dispatch of the notice, unless the contracting authority has published a prior information notice – in which case this period may be reduced to not less than 36 days. Contract documents are to be sent within 6 days of receipt of a request from any contractor, provided that they are requested by the date in the contract notice, and that any fee specified in the notice accompanies the request. Further information reasonably requested by the contractor, provided that the request is received in sufficient time, must be supplied not later than 6 days before the final date for the receipt of tenders. If contract documents are too bulky to be supplied within 6 days, or it is necessary that contractor be given the opportunity to inspect the site or documents relating to the contract documents (i.e. supporting documents), then the period of 52 (or 36) days for receipt of tenders must be extended to allow for inspection.

In order to decide on whom to award a contract the authority must apply certain selection and award criteria (as to which see below).

The restricted procedure

The restricted procedure is set out in regulation 12. As soon as possible after forming the intention to seek offers in relation to a public works contract, the authority must send a notice, in a form substantially corresponding to that set out in Part C of Schedule 2, to the *Official Journal*. The form contains prescribed information, broadly similar to that required for an open procedure notice, including the name and address of the authority, nature of contract, nature and extent of the services to be provided and general nature of the work, final date for receipt of requests to participate, and main terms as to financing. The last date for receipt of requests to be selected to tender may not be less than

37 days from the date of dispatch of the notice; this period may be reduced to 15 days where 37 days would be impracticable for reasons of urgency.

An authority cannot refuse to consider an application to be invited to tender by telegram, telex, facsimile or telephone, provided that it is confirmed by letter dispatched before the last date for receipt of applications.

The number of persons invited to tender must be sufficient to ensure genuine competition. But the authority can limit its choice of those invited to tender to a predetermined range, provided that: the lowest number in the range is no less than 5 and the highest no more than 20; the range is determined in the light of the nature of the work to be carried out under the contract; and the range is specified in the notice.

There is no time limit for the authority to choose its shortlist of candidates, but it must send invitations to tender simultaneously to each of the suppliers selected to tender. Certain information must be included in the invitation to tender (see regulation 12(10)). This information is largely of a kind that in the open procedure is put in the notice at the outset, and includes: the address to which requests for contract documents and further information relating to them should be sent, final date for making such a request and the fee; final date for receipt of tenders, the address to which they are to be sent, and the language in which they are to be drawn; a reference to the contract notice; an indication of the information to be included with the tender which may be required in connection with the contractor selection criteria; and the award criteria, if not specified in the contract notice.

The last date for receipt of tenders must be not less than 40 days from the dispatch of the invitation. This period must be extended if contractors have to inspect the site or supporting documents, and it may be curtailed to a period not less than 26 days if a prior information notice was published. If compliance with these periods is rendered impracticable for reasons of urgency, a period of not less then 10 days may be substituted (in which case the invitation must be sent by the most rapid means possible).

Further information relating to the contract documents, reasonably requested by a contractor, must be supplied not less than 6 days before the final date for receipt of tenders, but this period can be reduced to not less than 4 days where a longer period is impracticable for reasons of urgency.

The negotiated procedure

The negotiated procedure is set out in regulation 13. The procedure takes two forms: with publication of a notice in the *Official Journal*, and without publication. In the latter case other formalities are dispensed with as well. The procedure without publication can be used when:

- the open or restricted procedure was discontinued – provided that the contracting authority invites to negotiate the contract every contractor who submitted a tender (not being an excluded one) under those procedures;
- there were inappropriate or no tenders under the other procedures;
- for technical or artistic reasons, or because of exclusive rights, only particular persons can carry out the work;
- because of urgency the time limits in the other procedures cannot be met;
- additional works are necessary;
- repetition works need to be done.

In all other cases a notice must be published. Therefore it follows that a notice is obligatory when:

- it is not proposed to invite to negotiate the contract every contractor who submitted a tender under the other procedures;
- the reason for using the negotiated procedure is because the contract is purely for research experimental or development works (not to establish viability or recoup costs);
- the reason for using the negotiated procedure is that prior overall pricing is impossible.

If publication of a notice is necessary, the procedure is as follows. As soon as possible after forming the intention to seek offers the authority must send a notice in a form substantially corresponding to that set out in Part D of Schedule 2 inviting requests to be selected to negotiate. In the notice, the last date for receipt of the requests must be specified, and may not be less than 37 days from the date of dispatch of the notice. Where that minimum period is impracticable for reasons of urgency the authority may substitute a period of not less than 15 days, but in that event invitations to negotiate must be sent by the most rapid means possible. The authority is obliged to consider applications sent by letter, or by telegram, telex, facsimile or telephone if confirmed by a letter dispatched before the last date for receipt of applications. Where there is a sufficient number of persons who are suitable to be selected to negotiate the number selected must not be less than three.

In any event, whether a notice must be published in the *Official Journal* or not, the selection of suppliers and criteria for excluding suppliers must be in accordance with the selection criteria as set out in regulations 14–17.

Selection criteria

In order to decide who shall be awarded a contract, an authority must apply certain award criteria (see regulation 20). But before the buyer can place a contract he must first consider the standing of the contractor: that is, whether he has the capacity to perform the contract, whether he is solvent, and whether he is trustworthy. The authority may exclude a contractor from consideration only if one of the criteria for rejection of suppliers in regulation 14 applies (these include bankruptcy, insolvency, and serious misrepresentation), or if he does not meet the standards of economic and financial standing or technical capacity set by the authority and assessed in accordance with regulations 15 and 16.

The factors that a contracting authority can take into account in measuring the standing of a contractor are referred to in Title IV of the Works Directive as the 'criteria for qualitative selection'. The selection criteria set out in regulations 14–16 of the

Regulations are practically identical to those set out in the Supplies and Services Directives, namely:

- bankruptcy and insolvency;

- a criminal offence relating to the conduct of, or an act of grave misconduct in the course of, the business or profession;

- failure to fulfil obligations relating to social security contributions or other taxes;

- serious misrepresentation in supplying information needed for the application of the selection criteria;

- if the supplier is not registered on a professional or trade register;

- failure to meet minimum standards of economic and financial standing set by the contracting authority;

- failure to meet minimum standards of technical capacity set by the contracting authority.

In most Member States there is an obligation register on an appropriate trade register, such as the German Handelsregister or Handwerksrolle. In the common law countries there are no such registers: hence regulation 14(5) provides that a supplier established in the United Kingdom or Ireland shall be treated as registered on such a trade register if he is established in Ireland and certified as registered with the Registrar of Friendly Societies or is established in either State and is either certified as registered with the Registrar of Friendly Societies or is established in either State and is either certified as incorporated by the Registrar of Companies or is certified as having declared on oath that he is carrying on business in the trade in question in the State in which he is established at a specific place of business and under a specific trading name. And, for countries other than the United Kingdom and Ireland that have equivalent registers not listed in the regulations, or no registers, there is provision for the production of a certificate that the supplier is registered on an equivalent register, or for a declaration to be made on oath (see regulation 14(6) as substituted by the Public Supply Contracts Regulations 1995).

Provision of information

The Regulations limit the scope of the inquiry into the standing of a contractor. With regard to the reasons for rejecting contractors set out in regulation 14, the contracting authority may require such information as it needs, except that for some matters (bankruptcy and insolvency, criminal offences, social security or other taxes) an extract from the judicial record or a document issued by the relevant judicial or administrative authority, or the relevant competent authority in relation to taxes, is to be regarded as conclusive evidence that the contractor does not fall within the grounds for exclusion. For the United Kingdom, and other countries where there is no machinery for the issue of such documents, there is provision for the making of a declaration on oath.

Regulation 15 contains rules on the kind of information that the buyer can ask for when assessing whether a supplier meets any minimum standards of economic and financial standing that he requires of suppliers. A contracting authority may take account of some or all of the following:

- statements from the supplier's bankers;

- statements of, or extracts from, accounts where publication is required by the law of the Relevant State where the supplier is established (such as accounts published under the Companies Acts);

- a statement of overall turnover and the turnover in respect of works in the three previous financial years of the contractor.

Where this information is not appropriate, the authority may require other information, but whatever is required must be specified in the contract notice or invitation to tender. A supplier who is unable, for a valid reason, to provide the information that the authority requires can provide other information, because the authority must accept such other information as it considers appropriate.

There is a limit on the information as to technical capacity that the authority may demand of a supplier. Five categories of information are listed in regulation 16, which reproduces article

27 of the Directive; the information required by the contracting authority must be specified in the contract notice. The following is a summary of the information that can be demanded:

- a list of the qualifications of the contractor, of managerial staff or of those persons responsible for carrying out the work;

- a list of works carried out over the past 5 years, together with certificates of satisfactory completion;

- a statement of the tools, plant and technical equipment available to carry out the work;

- a statement of the contractor's average annual manpower and the number of managerial staff over the previous 3 years;

- a statement of the technicians or technical services that the contractor may call upon.

The authority may require supplementary information to that supplied under regulations 14 to 16, to clarify that information, and provided that it relates to the matters in those regulations.

The Directives preclude Member States from requiring a tenderer to furnish proof of his good standing and qualifications by means other than those set out in the Directives. In Case 76/81 *Transporoute et Travaux SA* v. *Minister of Public Works* [1982] ECR 417, [1982] 3 CMLR 382 the Luxembourg government invited tenders for works on the motorway at Arlon. The contract was awarded to a Luxembourg contractor, but Transporoute complained that it had put in the lowest bid. It was said that the decision was justified because Transporoute did not have an establishment certificate as required by the law of Luxembourg. The European Court rejected this contention, holding that the Belgian certificate produced by Transporoute was sufficient. The decision was justified not only by the words of the Directive, but also by article 59 of the EC Treaty, which guarantees the freedom to provide services within the Community.

Official lists

The official lists mentioned in regulation 18 have nothing to do with the kind of list that is drawn up as part of a prequalification system. In the Utilities Regulations there are rules about lists of suppliers because utilities operate a vendor qualification system, but the rules in the Works Regulations have to do only with suppliers meeting formal minimum requirements. Where a supplier is registered on the official lists of recognised contractors, in a Member State that maintains such lists, a certificate of registration must be accepted as evidence that the supplier meets most of the criteria for selection. The authority may not ask for supplementary information on matters covered by the certificate. Official lists do not operate in the United Kingdom.

In Case 389/92 *Ballast Nedam Groep NV* v. *Belgian State* [1994] ECR I-1289, [1994] 2 CMLR 836, the Belgian Minister of Public Works refused to include Ballast Nedam on the Belgian list of registered contractors because it was merely a holding company. It did not carry out works itself, but through the agency of its subsidiaries. The case was referred to the European Court, where it was held that the Works Directive must be interpreted in such a way as to permit account to be taken of companies belonging to the group, provided that the holding company was able to establish that it actually had available the resources of those companies.

Consortia

The basis of decision in the *Ballast Nedam* case (above) is that it is not necessary for the contractor to be a legal person in order to tender for a public contract. Regulation 19 provides that a contracting authority cannot refuse to consider a tender merely because a candidate is a consortium. It can, however, require the consortium to form a legal entity before entering into, or as a term of, a contract. A *consortium* means two or more persons, at least one of whom is a contractor, acting jointly for the purpose of being awarded a public works contract.

The award criteria

A contracting authority must award its contract either on the basis of the offer that is the most economically advantageous to the contracting authority, or on that which offers the lowest price. Where the criterion is the lowest price the contract must go to the lowest tender; no other criteria can be considered, nor may variations be entertained.

When an authority intends to base the award on the most economically advantageous offer, the criteria must be stated, preferably in descending order, in the contract notice or contract documents. The criteria that it may use to determine that an offer is the most economically advantageous include the following:

- price
- period for completion
- running costs
- profitability
- technical merit

An authority can take account of an offer containing variations provided that the offer meets its minimum requirements, which it has stated, together with any specific requirements for making such an offer, in the contract documents. If the authority will not consider variations it must say so in the contract notice; but the regulation makes no requirement to state that it will consider variations when that is the case.

A contracting authority may not reject a tender on the grounds that it has been drawn up with European specifications, or British technical specifications, which comply with Council directives on harmonisation or relate to design and method of calculation and execution of work and use of materials and goods (see regulation 20(5)).

Special rules apply to the rejection of an abnormally low offer; it may be rejected (even if price was the only basis of the award), but only if the authority has requested an explanation in writing. If price is the only basis of the award then the authority must examine the details of all the offers made and take into account any explanation given to it of the abnormally low tender; if economic advantage is the basis, then it must take into account any such explanation in assessing economic advantage. Explanations relating to the economy of the construction method, technical solutions suggested by the contractor or exceptionally favourable conditions available to the contractor, or the originality of the works, may all be taken into account. But, if an offer is rejected as abnormally low, a report must be sent to the Treasury, for onward transmission to the Commission.

The provisions on abnormally low offers reflect the decisions in Case 76/81 *Transporoute SA* v. *Minister of Public Works* [1982] ECR 417, [1982] 3 CMLR 382, and Case 31/87 *Gebroeders Bentjes* v. *Netherlands* [1988] ECR 4625, [1990] 1 CMLR 287.

When one part of a contracting authority is invited by another to compete with outside offers, the rules permit the acceptance of in-house bids. An offer includes a bid by one part of a contracting authority to carry out works for another part.

Subcontractors

Subcontractors are likely to execute the bulk of the work done under a works contract. The main contractor does not normally need to advertise subcontracts in the *Official Journal*, but in the case of a public works concession contract special rules apply. These rules are set out in regulation 26, as to which see below.

Award notices

An authority that has awarded a contract must, no later than 48 days after the award, send to the *Official Journal* a notice substantially corresponding to the form set out in Part E of Schedule 2 making known the result. Information that might impede law enforcement or otherwise be contrary to public interest, or might prejudice commercial interests or fair competition, need not be included.

Information about contract award procedures

Within 15 days of the date on which it receives a request from any unsuccessful contractor, the authority must inform the contractor of the reasons why he was unsuccessful and the name of the person awarded the contract. The contracting authority has to keep a record, in relation to each contract awarded, of the main particulars of the award (as listed in regulation 22(2)). The

Commission may require this information to be sent to it via the Treasury. Where an authority decides neither to award a contract nor to seek new offers, it must inform the *Official Journal* and (if asked) any contractors who either submitted offers, or asked to participate in the tenders or to negotiate for the contract.

Subsidised works contracts

Sometimes a contracting authority must impose, upon a body that it is subsidising, a condition that it comply with the Regulations (see regulation 23). The obligation arises when the following conditions apply:

- The contracting authority undertakes to contribute more than half the consideration for a contract.

- The contract would be a public works contract if the subsidised body were a contracting authority.

- The contract is entered into by a person (the 'subsidised body') other than a contracting authority.

- The contract is for the carrying out of any of the activities in Group 502 of the General Classification of Economic Activities in the EC (construction of roads bridges railways etc.) or for the carrying out of building work for hospitals, sports recreation and leisure facilities, school and university buildings or buildings for administrative purposes.

In such a case the authority must make it a condition that the subsidised body comply with the provisions of the Regulations as if it were a contracting authority, and must ensure that the subsidised body either does so or repays the contribution.

Public housing schemes

Regulation 24 is the only regulation in the Works Regulations that recognises that it is not always wise to treat the contractor as an adversary who must be pitted against all comers, and that a partnership is sometimes preferable when the relationship is long term and involves close collaboration and commitment. For a public housing scheme, where the size and complexity of the scheme and the estimated duration of the works require that the planning of the scheme be based on the close collaboration of a team comprising representatives of the authority, experts and the contractor, a contracting authority may depart from the Regulations insofar as it is necessary to select the contractor who is most suitable for integration into the team. Nevertheless, the authority must comply with the rules of the restricted procedure to the extent of publishing a notice (including an accurate job description) in the *Official Journal* and applying the contractor selection criteria.

Public works concession contracts

A public works concession contract is defined as a public works contract under which the consideration given by the contracting authority consists of or includes the grant of a right to exploit the work or works to be carried out under the contract. A contracting authority must publicise its intention to seek offers in relation to such a contract by means of a notice corresponding to that set out in Part F of Schedule 2. The date for the receipt of tenders or requests to be selected to tender for or negotiate the contract must not be less than 52 days from the date of dispatch of the notice.

Complicated rules apply to subcontracts for works to be carried out under a public works concession contract: see regulation 25. A contracting authority seeking offers in relation to a concession contract must either request, in the invitation to tender, the contractor to specify the proportion that he intends to subcontract, or require, as a term of the contract, that he subcontract not less than 30% of the value of the work. Subcontracts to affiliates of the concessionaire are not included in the calculation, and the percentage required to be subcontracted can be higher at the discretion of the authority; the value of the work is taken to be the value of the consideration that the authority would give were it not granting a concession contract.

Where a concessionaire is a contracting authority it must comply with the Works Regulations when it places subcontracts for the work or works to be carried out under a concession contract. When the concessionaire is not a contracting authority it must, for some kinds of contracts, send a notice to the *Official Journal* and comply with the procedures set out in regulation 26(3). The contracts affected are those to which the following conditions apply:

- subcontracts, not with affiliates, for work or works to be carried out under the concession contract,

- which would, if the the concessionaire were a contracting authority, be a public works contract – other than one for which the negotiated procedure pursuant to regulation 10(2)(d) to (h) could be used.

Paragraphs (d) to (h) of regulation 10(2) cover situations where there are inappropriate or no tenders under the other procedures, exclusive rights, urgency, additional works or repetition works.

When the contract is one of the kinds where the concessionaire is bound to follow the procedure in regulation 26(3) he is obliged to publish a notice in a form substantially corresponding to that set out in Part G of Schedule 2. If the notice invites tenders the last date for receipt must be not less than 40 days from the date of dispatch of the notice. If the notice invites applications to be selected to tender or negotiate then the last date for the receipt of such applications must not be less than 37 days from the dispatch of the notice, and the last date for receipt of tenders (following selection of those invited to tender) must be not less than 40 days from the date of dispatch of the invitation. In each case the final date must be specified in the notice or invitation as the case may be.

Affiliates

When a concessionaire is required to subcontract a proportion of the work, contracts with affiliates are not included in the calculation. A concessionaire who is not a contracting authority need not publish a contract notice in the case of a subcontract with an affiliate. And a contracting authority must require applicants for a concession contract to submit a list of all the persons affiliated to the applicant, and update it from time to time. It is therefore important to understand the term 'affiliate', and this is defined in regulation 26(5).

The main factors indicating that a person is to be treated as an affiliate of another are that he exercises a dominant influence over the other person, or that both are members of a consortium formed for the purpose of performing the concession contract. A person is taken to exercise a dominant influence over another if he possesses a greater part of the issued share capital or controls the voting power attached to that greater part, or may appoint more than half the individuals responsible for management.

Employment protection and working conditions

A contracting authority that includes information as to where the contractor may obtain information about obligations relating to employment protection and working conditions which will apply to the works carried out under the contract must request contractors to indicate that they have taken those obligations into account in preparing their tender, or in negotiating the contract (see regulation 27).

Reports

A contracting authority is obliged to send a report to the Treasury every alternate year, specifying for the year preceding the year in which the report is made the consideration for each public works contract, the procedure used, if the negotiated procedure was used the grounds for so doing, the category of works under the contract, and the nationality of the person to whom it was awarded. Reports containing other information needed by the Treasury for the purpose of informing the Commission may also be required (see regulation 28).

If the authority is not a minister or a government department, reports must be sent to the minister most closely connected with the functions of the contracting authority, and it is his responsibility to pass it on to the Treasury.

Chapter 7

Public Service Contracts

The purchasing of services in the public sector is governed by the Services Directive, Council Directive 92/50 relating to the coordination of procedures for the award of public service contracts (OJ L209 24.7.92 p1), implemented in the United Kingdom by the Public Services Contracts Regulations 1993 (SI 1993/3228), which also implements, insofar as is relevant, the Compliance Directive 89/665 (OJ L395 30.12.89 p33). The Services Directive was drafted in such a way as to accord as closely as possible with the Supplies and Public Works directives.

Application

The preamble to the Directive indicates that for the time being the full application of the Directive must be limited to those sevices where its provisions will enable the full potential for increased cross-frontier trade to be realised, whereas contracts for other services need to be monitored before a decision is taken on the full application of the Directive. The Regulations sometimes apply in their entirety and sometimes apply to a limited extent, depending upon the nature of the proposed service contract; the Directive calls this *two-tier application*.

The categories of services to which the Regulations apply are set out in Schedule 1, which is divided into two parts: Part A and Part B. Whenever a contracting authority seeks offers in relation to a proposed Part A services contract, other than one excluded by regulations 6 or 7, the regulations apply in their entirety. But in relation to a proposed Part B services contract (sometimes

known as *residual services*) other than one excluded by regulations 6 or 7, only Parts I and VII and regulations 8, 22, 27(2), 28
and 29 apply. The practical effect of this is that if the contract is a
Part B services contract then although technical specifications
must be drawn up in terms of European specifications as far as
possible, and an award notice must be published, there is no
requirement to use the open, restricted or negotiated procedures
set out in the Regulations. There remains, however, an obligation
to make statistical reports if required under regulation 27(2).

Article 10 of the Directive provides that when contracts have
as their objects services listed in parts A and B, the full regime
applies if the value of the services in part A is greater than those
in part B.

In the Directive *contracting authorities* are defined as the State,
regional or local authorities, bodies governed by public law, and
associations formed by one or several such authorities or bodies
governed by public law. There is a definition in the Directive of a
'body governed by public law', but for States where the concept
is unknown the Directive refers to a list of bodies and categories
of bodies that fulfil the necessary criteria, which is set out in
Annex I of Works Directive 93/37/EEC. The easiest way to
understand the definition as it applies in the United Kingdom is
to refer to regulation 3 of the Regulations. This contains the list of
bodies taken from the Works Directive. Most government
departments and organisations are included. Associations
formed by one or more such bodies, such as joint ventures
between two or more contracting authorities and companies
formed by a contracting authority, would come within the
definition.

Regulation 3(1)(r) contains the broader category of a corporation or group appointed to act for the specific purpose of
meeting needs in the general interest and not having an industrial or commercial character. This is derived from the definition
of a body governed by public law to be found in the Directive:
that is, established for the specific purpose of meeting needs in
the general interest, not having an industrial or commercial
character, having a legal personality, and financed for the most
part by the State, or local authorities, or other bodies governed
by public law, or subject to management supervision by those
bodies, or having an administrative, managerial or supervisory

board, more than half of whose members are appointed by the State, regional or local authorities or other bodies governed by public law. What is important to this definition is State control or finance.

Exclusions

Procurement rules are inappropriate or impractical for some kinds of services: therefore the list of general exclusions set out in regulation 6 is longer than in the case of the other Regulations. The first three exclusions set out below are common to all the Regulations. In summary, the contracts excluded from the Services Regulations are:

- secret or security contracts;
- defence contracts to which the provisions of article 223 of the EC Treaty apply;
- contracts governed by international agreements;
- contracts for the acquisition of land or interests in land;
- contracts for the acquisition, development or production of programme material for radio or televison by a broadcaster, or for purchase of broadcast time;
- voice telephony, telex, radiopaging or satellite services;
- arbitration or conciliation services;
- contracts for financial services in connection with the issue, purchase, sale, or transfer of securities or other financial instruments;
- contracts for research and development, unless the benefits accrue exclusively to the authority for its own use and the services are to be wholly paid for by the contracting authority;
- contracts under which services are provided by another contracting authority (this includes an authority in another Relevant State) because it has an exclusive right to provide (or must have the right in order to provide) the services.

Thresholds

The Regulations do not apply to the seeking of offers in relation to a proposed public services contract where the estimated value of the contract (net of value added tax) at the relevant time is less than the appropriate threshold. In the case of subcentral government entities the threshold is 200,000 ECU, fixed at the sterling equivalent of £158,018 for the period of probably 2 years from January 1996. In the case of central government purchases (the GATT, now GPA, authorities listed in Schedule 1 of the Supplies Regulations), the threshold is 130,000 SDR as a result of the Government Purchasing Agreement, fixed at the sterling equivalent of £108,667 for a similar period.

The *relevant time* (see regulation 7(12)) means the date on which a contract notice would be sent to the *Official Journal* if the requirement to send such a notice applied to the contract: in other words, as soon as possible after forming the intention to seek offers in relation to the contract. The *estimated value* is the value of the consideration that the authority expects to give under the contract. In determining this amount the authority must include the premium payable for insurance services, fees and commissions for banking and financial services, and fees or commissions for design services. With regard to banking and other financial services the Directive says that interest as well as other types of remuneration must be taken into account, but these words are not reproduced in the Regulations.

Aggregation

The rules on thresholds cannot be circumvented by splitting a large contract into smaller contracts. The usual rule is that where a contracting authority has a single requirement for services, and a number of public services contracts are entered into to fulfil the requirement, the value of each is taken to be the value of the whole. The authority must take the aggregate of the value of the consideration that it expects to give under each of the contracts.

But the contracting authority may, if it chooses, make an exception and treat a contract as worth less than the threshold if it is worth less than 80,000 ECU (£63,207), provided that the total value of the contracts treated in this way is not more than 20% of the value of the consideration for the whole requirement. A similar system is used in the Works Regulations; see Chapter 6.

Where a contracting authority has a requirement over a period of time and for that purpose enters into a series of contracts or a contract that under its terms is renewable, then the estimated value of a component contract is taken to be either the aggregate value of similar contracts over the previous 12 months (or financial year), or the estimated value of those expected to be placed in the next 12 months. See paragraph (7) of regulation 7 for the detail of how this system works. As much as an authority may not split contracts, so it may not choose a valuation method in accordance with paragraph (7) in order to avoid the Regulations.

Where services are to be provided over a period exceeding 4 years, or over an indefinite period, the value of the contract is taken to be 48 times the value that the authority expects to give each month. Where a contract includes options, the value is taken to be the highest possible consideration that could be given under the contract.

Technical specifications

If a purchasing authority wishes to lay down technical specifications for services under a public services contract, and for goods and materials used, it must specify all of them in the contract documents, and as a rule it must use European standards if they exist. Regulation 8 of the Services Regulations deals with these requirements; regulation 8 of the Supplies Regulations, regulation 8 of the Works Regulations, and regulation 11 of the Utilities Regulations are in substantially the same terms.

Normally technical specifications must be defined by reference to any relevant European specifications. *European specification* means a common technical specification, a British standard implementing a European standard, or a European technical approval. A *common technical specification* means a technical specification drawn up in accordance with a procedure recognised by the Member States with a view to uniform application in all Member States, which has been published in the *Official*

Journal. European technical approvals are not yet available: therefore the normal technical specification will be a British standard implementing a European standard, identified by its prefix 'BS EN'.

A list of the circumstances in which an authority may depart from European specifications is set out in paragraph (4) of regulation 8. They may be summarised as follows:

- *Mandatory requirements*
  Where the the utility is obliged to define the technical specifications by reference to technical requirements that are mandatory under United Kingdom law and not incompatible with EC law.

- *Impossibility*
  Where either the European specifications do not include provision for, or it is technically impossible to establish conformity to, the European specifications.

- *Telecommunications, IT and other Community obligations*
  Where use of European specifications would conflict with Council Directive 91/263/EEC, Council Decision 87/95/EEC, and other Community obligations relating to specific types of services, material or goods.

- *Incompatibility*
  Where it would oblige the authority to use material or goods incompatible with equipment already in use, or would entail disproportionate costs or technical difficulties.

- *Innovation*
  Where the project is genuinely innovative, so that European standards would be inappropriate.

If a contracting authority proposes to rely on any of the above it must state in the contract notice which circumstance it relies on, or if that is impossible it must specify the circumstance in the contract documents. In any event it must keep a record. If the Commission or a relevant State so require, this record must be sent to the Commission via the Treasury; it is a part of the machinery by which the Commission can operate the corrective mechanism of the Directive. Although a departure from

European standards is allowed on the grounds of incompatibility with equipment in use, costs, or technical difficulties, the authority may do so only when it has a clearly defined and recorded strategy for changing over, within a fixed period, to European specifications.

There is a hierarchy to the specifications that may be used. First come any relevant European specifications, but in their absence the authority must use British technical specifications recognised as complying with the basic requirements specified in any Council Directives on technical harmonisation, in particular Council Directive 89/106/EEC, which relates to standards and technical approvals for construction products. The authority may use British technical specifications relating to design and method of calculation and execution of work or works and use of materials and goods. Technical specifications may also be defined by reference to British standards implementing international standards; other British standards and technical approvals; or any other standards.

In practice the process is as follows. The buyer must first consider whether there is a relevant European specification: that is, a United Kingdom standard implementing a European standard, a common technical specification, or a European technical approval. If a European specification exists it must be used unless one of the exceptions in regulation 8(4) applies (mandatory requirements; technical impossibility; conflict with IT standards directives; incompatibility; or innovation). If the exception is incompatibility, there must be a recorded strategy to change to European standards. In the absence of a European specification the following conditions apply. The buyer must define the technical specifications in the contract documents by reference to British technical specifications recognised as complying with the basic requirements specified in any Council Directives on technical harmonisation, in particular Council Directive 89/106/EEC (OJ L140 11.2.89 p12). The buyer may use British technical specifications relating to design and method of calculation of work or works and use of materials and goods. The buyer may use British standards implementing international standards; failing that, other British standards and technical approvals; and failing that, the buyer may use any other standards.

Contract documents may not include technical specifications that refer to goods of a specific make or source or to a particular process, and which have the effect of favouring or eliminating particular service providers. References to trademarks, patents, types, origin or means of production may not be incorporated into the technical specifications in the contract documents. However, paragraph 10 contains a proviso that permits the use of such references if such references are justified by the subject of the contract, or if the subject of the contract cannot otherwise be described by reference to technical specifications that are sufficiently precise and intelligible to all service providers, provided that references are accompanied by the words 'or equivalent'.

Prior indicative notice

Contracting authorities have to make known their purchasing requirement as soon as possible after the beginning of their budgetary year by means of an indicative notice showing the intended total procurement in each of the service categories, listed in Schedule 1 Part A of the Regulations, which they envisage awarding during the subsequent 12 months. The requirement is implemented by regulation 9, and the form of the notice is set out in Schedule 2 Part A of the Regulations. The obligation to publish an indicative notice does not apply to contracts that are excluded from the Regulations by regulation 6 (general exclusions) or regulation 7 (thresholds). Neither is there any obligation to publish an indicative notice if the total consideration under all the proposed contracts for the provision of services within the same category specified in Part A is expected to be less than 750,000 ECU (fixed at the sterling equivalent of £592,568).

Procedures

The procedures that must be used in relation to public services contracts are set out in Part III of the Regulations. The main requirements are that when seeking offers an authority must use one of three procedures: the open procedure, whereby any person who is interested may submit a tender; the restricted procedure, whereby only those persons selected by the contracting authority may submit tenders; and the negotiated procedure, whereby the contracting authority negotiates the terms of the contract with one or more persons selected by it. There is a free choice in the use of the first two procedures, but the negotiated procedure may be used only in exceptional cases. Each of these procedures involves the publication of notices in the *Official Journal,* and there are stipulated minimum periods of time for service providers to ask for information, make offers in response to notices, and so on. The forms of these notices are set out in Schedule 2 of the Regulations. Any notice required to be sent to the *Official Journal* must be sent by the most appropriate means to the Office for Official Publications of the European Communities (see further Chapter 2).

The process of making an award involves three stages: the selection of the appropriate award procedure and publication of a notice; the selection of service providers who can compete for the award; and the making of the award.

Choice of award procedure

Unless exceptional circumstances justify the use of the negotiated procedure, a purchasing authority must use either the open or restricted procedure (there is a free choice between the two) for the purpose of seeking offers in relation to a proposed services contract; in practice most contracts are placed by means of the restricted procedure. The circumstances in which the negotiated procedure may be used are set out in regulation 10, and may be summarised as when:

- the open or restricted procedure was discontinued
  - because of irregular tenders, or
  - because the tenders were excluded after they were evaluated under the open or restricted procedures;

- prior overall pricing is impossible;

- the specification cannot be drawn up with precision (in particular, intellectual and financial services);

- there were inappropriate or no tenders under the other procedures;

- for technical or artistic reasons, or because of exclusive rights, only particular persons can carry out the work;

- there is a design contest, provided that all the successful contestants are invited to negotiate;

- because of urgency the time limits in the other procedures cannot be met;

- additional services are necessary (but no more than 50% of the main contract);

- repetition services are wanted (these must be a repetition of services provided under the original contract, and in accordance with the project for the purpose of which the first contract was entered into).

A number of conditions apply to the above exceptions. In the case of irregular, excluded or absent tenders the contract placed by negotiated procedure must be substantially the same as that which was proposed in the abortive open or restricted procedures (see regulation 10(3)). *Irregular tenders* include tenders that fail to meet the contract specifications, offer impermissible variations, or fail to meet technical specifications. If the reason for the use of the negotiated procedure is that there are no tenders, then a report must, if the the Commission requests it, be submitted to the Treasury for onward transmission to the Commission.

There is no exception analogous to that for research, experimental or development works to be found in the Works Regulations.

The negotiated procedure may be used in cases of extreme urgency, where the time limits under the Regulations cannot be met, but only where this is strictly necessary, and the urgency must be brought about by events unforeseeable by, and not attributable to, the contracting authority.

When a contracting authority wants a service provider to provide additional services the need must, likewise, arise through unforeseen circumstances, and either there must be technical or economic reasons why the additional services cannot be carried out separately from the services under the original contract, or the services must be strictly necessary for the performance of that contract. However, the value of contracts for additional services must not in aggregate exceed 50% of the value of the the original contract.

The open procedure

The open procedure is set out in regulation 11, which is in terms substantially the same as those of the equivalent regulation in the Supplies Regulations and Works Regulations. As soon as possible after forming the intention to seek offers in relation to a public supply contract, the authority must send a notice to the *Official Journal*, in a form substantially corresponding to that set out in Part B of Schedule 2. The form contains prescribed information, including the name and address of the authority, category of services and description, CPC reference number, and main terms as to financing.

The final date for receipt of tenders must be specified in the notice, and may be not less than 52 days from the date of dispatch of the notice, unless the contracting authority has published a prior information notice – in which case the period may be reduced to not less than 36 days. Contract documents are to be sent within 6 days of receipt of a request from any contractor, provided that they are requested in good time and any fee specified in the notice accompanies the request. Further information reasonably requested by the contractor, provided that the request is received in sufficient time, must be supplied not later than 6 days before the final date for the receipt of tenders. If contract documents are too bulky to be supplied within these periods, or if it is necessary to give service providers the opportunity to inspect the site or documents relating to the contract documents (i.e. supporting documents), then the period of 52 (or 36) days for receipt of tenders must be extended to allow for inspection.

The restricted procedure

The restricted procedure is set out in regulation 12, and is in terms practically identical to those of the equivalent regulation in the Works Regulations and the Supplies Regulations. As soon as possible after forming the intention to seek offers in relation to a public works contract the authority must send a notice to the *Official Journal*, in a form substantially corresponding to that set out in Part C of Schedule 2. The form contains prescribed information, broadly similar to that required for an open procedure notice. The last date for receipt of requests to be selected to tender must be specified in the notice, and may not be less than 37 days from the date of dispatch of the notice; this period may be reduced to 15 days where 37 days would be impracticable for reasons of urgency.

In making its selection, and in issuing invitations to tender, the contracting authority must not discriminate on the grounds of nationality of the relevant State in which the tenderers are established. Provided that it is confirmed by letter dispatched before the last date for receipt of applications, an authority cannot refuse to consider an application to be invited to tender sent by telegram, telex, facsimile or telephone.

The number of persons invited to tender must be sufficient to ensure genuine competition. But the authority can limit its choice of those invited to tender to a predetermined range, provided that: the lowest number in the range is not less than 5 and the highest no more than 20; the range is determined in the light of the nature of the services to be carried out under the contract; and the range is specified in the notice.

There is no time limit for the authority to choose its shortlist of candidates, but it must send invitations to tender simultaneously to each of the suppliers selected to tender. Certain information must be included in the invitation to tender (see regulation 12(10)). This information is largely of a kind that in the open procedure is put into the notice at the outset, and includes: the address to which requests for contract documents and further information relating to them should be sent, the final date for making such a request and the fee; the final date for receipt of tenders, the address to which they are to be sent, and the language in which they are to be drawn; a reference to the contract notice; an indication of the information to be included with the tender which may be required in connection with the selection criteria; and the award criteria, if not specified in the contract notice.

The last date for receipt of tenders must be not less than 40 days from the dispatch of the invitation. This period must be extended if contractors have to inspect the site or supporting documents, and it may be curtailed to a period not less than 26 days if a prior information notice was published. If compliance with these periods is rendered impracticable for reasons of urgency, a period of not less then 10 days may be substituted (in which case the invitation must be sent by the most rapid means possible).

Further information relating to the contract documents, reasonably requested by a service provider, must be supplied not less than 6 days before the final date for receipt of tenders, but this period can be reduced to not less than 4 days where a longer period is impracticable for reasons of urgency.

The negotiated procedure

The negotiated procedure is set out in regulation 13, which is in substantially identical terms to the equivalent regulation in the Works Regulations and the Supply Regulations. The procedure takes two forms: with publication of a notice in the *Official Journal*, and without publication. In the latter case other formalities are dispensed with as well. The procedure without publication can be used when:

- the open or restricted procedure was discontinued – provided that the contracting authority invites to negotiate the contract every contractor who submitted a tender (not being an excluded one) under those procedures;

- there were inappropriate or no tenders under the other procedures;

- for technical or artistic reasons, or because of exclusive rights, only particular persons can provide the services;

- there is a design contest, provided that all the successful contestants are invited to negotiate;

- because of urgency the time limits in the other procedures cannot be met;

- additional services are necessary (for unforeseen circumstances not included in the project initially considered or in the original contract);

- repetition services are required.

A number of ancillary conditions apply to the above exceptions. In the case of irregular, excluded or absent tenders the contract placed by negotiated procedure must be substantially the same as that which was proposed in the abortive open or restricted procedures (see regulation 10(3)). *Irregular tenders* include tenders that fail to meet the contract specifications, offer impermissible variations, or fail to meet technical specifications. If the reason for the use of the negotiated procedure is that there are no tenders, then a report must, if the Commission requests, be submitted to the Treasury for onward transmission to the Commission. The negotiated procedure may be used in cases of extreme urgency, where the time limits under the Regulations cannot be met, but only where this is strictly necessary, and the urgency must be brought about by events unforeseeable by, and not attributable to, the contracting authority (see regulation 10(2)(g)). The exception in relation to additional services applies only if the services cannot for technical or economic reasons be provided separately, or if they are strictly necessary to the performance of the original contract, and the exception cannot be applied if the value of the additions exceeds 50% of the value of the contract. Particular care must be taken with the exception for repetition contracts, because the negotiated procedure cannot be used unless the contract notice for the original contract mentions the possibility that a new contract might be placed under the negotiated procedure. It is a condition also that the award procedure for the new contract must be begun within 3 years of placing the old contract.

If publication of a notice is necessary, the procedure is as follows. As soon as possible after forming the intention to seek offers the authority must send a notice to the *Official Journal* in a form substantially corresponding to that set out in Part D of Schedule 2, inviting requests to be selected to negotiate. In the notice, the last date for receipt of the requests must be specified, and may not be less than 37 days from the date of dispatch of the notice. Where that minimum period is impracticable for reasons of urgency, the authority may substitute a period of not less than 15 days, but in that event invitations to negotiate must be sent by the most rapid means possible. The authority is obliged to consider applications sent by letter, or by telegram, telex, facsimile or telephone if confirmed by a letter dispatched before the last date for receipt of applications. Where there is a sufficient number of persons who are suitable to be selected to negotiate, the number selected must not be less than three.

In any event, whether a notice must be published in the *Official Journal* or not, the selection of suppliers and criteria for excluding suppliers must be in accordance with the selection criteria as set out in regulations 14–17.

Selection criteria

Before the buyer can place a contract he must consider the standing of the seller: that is, whether the contractor has the capacity to perform the contract, whether he is solvent, and whether he is trustworthy. The factors that a contracting authority can take into account in measuring the standing of a contractor are referred to in Title VI of the Services Directive as the *criteria for qualitative selection*. Regulations 14–17 of the Services Regulations contain these so-called 'selection criteria'; they follow closely the equivalent regulations in the Works Regulations and Supply Regulations – save that the evidence of ability and technical capacity that can be required is different because of the nature of a service contract. A contracting authority may treat candidates as inelegible, or exclude them from its invitation to tender or negotiate, only if they fail on a ground specified in regulation 14, or do not satisfy minimum standards of economic and financial standing and technical capacity required of contractors by the contracting authority in accordance with regulations 15 and 16. In brief, the criteria for rejection of a provider of services are:

- bankruptcy and insolvency;

- a criminal offence relating to the conduct of, or an act of grave misconduct in the course of, the business or profession;

- failure to fulfil obligations relating to social security contributions or other taxes;

- serious misrepresentation in supplying information needed for the application of the selection criteria;

- if the service provider is not licensed, or not a member of an organisation (where the law of the State where he is established requires this);

- if the service provider is not registered on a professional or trade register;

- failure to meet minimum standards of economic and financial standing set by the contracting authority;

- failure to meet minimum standards of technical capacity set by the contracting authority.

In most member States there is an obligation register on an appropriate trade register, such as the German Handelsregister or Handwersrolle. In the common law countries there are no such registers: hence regulation 14(5) provides that a supplier established in the United Kingdom or Ireland shall be treated as registered on such a trade register if he is established in Ireland and certified as registered with the Registrar of Friendly Societies or is established in either State and is either certified as registered with the Registrar of Friendly Societies or is established in either State and is either certified as incorporated by the Registrar of Companies or is certified as having declared on oath (presumably by a commissioner for oaths – in other words in an affidavit) that he is carrying on business in the trade in question in the State in which he is established at a specific place of business and under a specific trading name. For countries other than the United Kingdom and Ireland that have equivalent registers not listed in the Regulations, or no registers, there is provision for the production of a certificate that the supplier is registered on an equivalent register, or for a declaration to be made on oath (see regulation 14(7), which is an amendment inserted by the Public Supply Contracts Regulations 1995).

Provision of information

The Regulations limit the scope of the inquiry into the standing of a contractor. With regard to the reasons for rejecting contractors set out in regulation 14, the contracting authority may require such information as it needs, except that for some matters (bankruptcy and insolvency, criminal offences, social security or other taxes) an extract from the judicial record or a document issued by the relevant judicial or administrative authority, or the relevant competent authority in relation to taxes, is to be regarded as conclusive evidence that the contractor does not fall within the ground for exclusion. For the United Kingdom, and other countries, where there is no machinery for the issue of such documents there is provision for the making of a declaration on oath.

Regulation 15 contains rules on the kind of information that the buyer can ask for when assessing whether a supplier meets any minimum standards of economic and financial standing that he requires of suppliers. A contracting authority may take account of some or all of the following:

- statements from the service provider's bankers, or evidence of professional risk indemnity insurance;

- statements of, or extracts from, accounts where publication is required by the law of the relevant state where the service provider is established (such as accounts published under the Companies Acts);

- a statement of overall turnover and the turnover in respect of relevant services in the three previous financial years.

Where this information is not appropriate the authority may require other information, but whatever is required must be specified in the contract notice or invitation to tender. A service provider who is unable, for a valid reason, to give the information that the authority requires can provide other information, because the authority must accept such other information as it considers appropriate.

There is a limit on the evidence of technical capacity that the authority may demand of a supplier. Article 32 of the Directive states that the ability of service providers to perform services may be evaluated in particular with regard to their skills, efficiency, experience and reliability. The information needed by the contracting authority in order to assess ability and technical capacity must be specified in the contract notice. The following is a summary of the information, listed in regulation 16, that the authority can take into account in assessing technical capacity:

- educational and professional qualifications of the contractor, of managerial staff or of those persons responsible for providing the services;

- services provided in the past 3 years, dates, consideration, certificates and declarations attesting the services provided;

- technicians or technical bodies involved, particularly if concerned with quality control;

- average annual manpower and number of managerial staff over the previous 3 years;

- tools, plant and equipment available;

- measures for ensuring quality, study and research facilities;

- where the services are complex or required for a special purpose, a check by the authority (or a competent official body on their behalf) on the technical capacity and, if relevant, on the study and research facilities and quality control measures of the service provider;

- any certificate that the services conform to BS 5750, or a certificate of a body conforming to the EN 45 000 European standards series attesting conformity to relevant quality assurance standards based on the EN 29 000 series, or equivalent evidence;

- any proportion of the contract to be subcontracted.

The authority may require information supplementary to that supplied under regulations 14–16, to clarify that information, and provided that it relates to the matters in those regulations. It should be noted, however, that there is a requirement under regulation 30 for a contracting authority to comply with such requirements as to confidentiality of information provided to it by a service provider as he may reasonably request. This is important when it comes to the award notice.

Official lists

The official lists mentioned in regulation 18 have nothing to do with the kind of list, drawn up as part of a prequalification system, which is mentioned in the Utilities Regulations; in the latter there are rules about such lists, because all utilities operate a vendor qualification system to screen potential suppliers. The rules in the Services Regulations have only to do with suppliers meeting certain formal minimum requirements. Where a service provider is registered on the official lists of recognised suppliers that some States maintain, a certificate of registration must, in relation to most of the criteria for selection, be accepted as evidence that the supplier meets the necessary conditions, and the authority is not entitled to ask for supplementary information on matters covered by the certificate. Official lists do not operate in the United Kingdom.

Consortia

It is not necessary for the supplier to be a legal person in order to tender for a public contract. Regulation 19 therefore provides that a *consortium* means 2 or more persons, at least one of whom is a service provider, acting jointly for the purpose of being awarded a public services contract. A contracting authority cannot refuse to consider a tender merely on the grounds that a service provider is a consortium; it can, however, require the consortium to form a legal entity before entering into or as a term of a contract. But a contracting authority may require a supplier to indicate in his tender what part of the contract he intends to subcontract to another person – see regulation 31.

Corporations

Under regulation 20 the contracting authority may not disqualify a tender on the grounds that the service provider must be an individual, corporation or other type of body under the law of the United Kingdom if under the law of the relevant State he is authorised to provide services. It may require a service provider that is not an individual to indicate the names and qualifications of the staff who will be responsible for providing the services. These provisions are not reflected in the Supplies Regulations.

Award criteria

A contracting authority must award its contract on the basis of either the offer that is the most economically advantageous to the contracting authority, or that which offers the lowest price. Where the basis of the award is to be the lowest price, the contract must go to the lowest tender; no other criteria can be considered, and variations cannot be entertained.

When an authority intends to base the award on the most economically advantageous offer, the criteria must be stated, preferably in descending order, in the contract notice or contract documents. The criteria that it may use to determine that an offer is the most economically advantageous include:

- period for completion or delivery

- quality

- aesthetic and functional characteristics

- technical merit

- after-sales service

- technical assistance

- price.

An authority can take account of an offer containing variations provided that the offer meets its minimum requirements, which it has stated, together with any specific requirements for making such an offer, in the contract documents. If the authority will not take notice of variations it must say so in the contract notice; but the regulation makes no requirement for the authority to say that it will consider variations when that is the case. A contracting authority may not reject a variation on the grounds that it would lead to the award of a public supply contract.

A contracting authority may not reject a tender on the ground that it has been drawn up with European specifications or British technical specifications that comply with Council directives on harmonisation or relate to design and method of calculation and execution of work and use of materials and goods (see regulation 21(6)).

Special rules apply to the rejection of an abnormally low offer; it may be rejected (even if price was the only basis of the award), but only if the authority has requested in writing an explanation. If price is the only basis of the award then the authority must examine the details of all the offers made and take into account any explanation given to it of the abnormally low tender; if economic advantage is the basis, then it must take into account any such explanation in assessing economic advantage. Explanations relating to the economy of the method, technical solutions suggested by the service provider or exceptionally favourable conditions, or the originality of the services proposed by the provider, may be taken into account. But if an offer is rejected as abnormally low, a report must be sent via the Treasury to the Commission.

When one part of a contracting authority is invited by another to compete with outside offers the rules permit the acceptance of in-house bids. An offer includes a bid by one part of a contracting authority to carry out services for another part.

Award notices

An authority that has awarded a contract, whether for Part A or Part B services, must, no later than 48 days after the award, send to the *Official Journal* a notice substantially corresponding to the form set out in Part E of Schedule 2 making known the result; if it is a Part B contract the authority must state whether or not it agrees to publication, because part B notices are not normally published and are used only for monitoring purposes. Information that might impede law enforcement or otherwise be contrary to public interest, or prejudice commercial interests or fair competition, need not be included.

Information about contract award procedures

Within 15 days of the date on which it receives a request from any unsuccessful service provider, the authority must inform the contractor of the reasons why he was unsuccessful and the name of the person awarded the contract. The contracting authority has to keep a record of the main particulars of each award (as listed in regulation 23(2)). If the Commission so requests, a report containing this information must be sent to the Treasury for onward transmission to the Commission. Where an authority decides neither to award a contract nor to seek new offers, it must inform the *Official Journal* and (if asked) anyone who submitted offers, or asked to participate in the tenders or negotiate for the contract.

Design contests

Design contests are popular in Continental Europe as a means of awarding contracts for such wonders as the Pompidou Centre. There is a fixed procedure for these competitions. The threshold is the same as that which applies to the other procedures: that is, 200,000 ECU (£158,018). The threshold applies both to the contract and to the prize, so that if the design contest is organised as part of a procedure leading to the award of a public services contract and the estimated value of any contract which it is intended to award as the outcome of the contract is worth not less than 200,000 ECU, the Regulations apply. But equally, whether or not it is organised as part of a procedure leading to the award of such a contract, if the aggregate value of the prizes or payments for the contest is not less than 200,000 ECU then the Regulations apply.

The contracting authority must publicise its intention to hold a design contest by sending a notice to the *Official Journal* in a form corresponding to that set out in Part F of Schedule 2. The rules of the contest must be made available to any service provider who wishes to participate. A contracting authority may restrict the number of persons invited to participate in a design contest, provided that this is done on the basis of clear and non-discriminatory criteria, and provided that it invites enough persons to ensure adequate competition.

Regulation 20 applies to design competitions as it does to the other procedures: that is, the contracting authority may not disqualify a competitor because he is not a corporation or some other kind of body if under the law of the relevant State in which he is established he is authorised to provide the services. But a competitor that is not an individual may be required to indicate the names and qualifications of the staff who will be responsible for providing the services.

The contracting authority must ensure that the jury makes its decision independently, and solely on the criteria set out in the notice. It has several duties designed to ensure fairness of the competition. The proposals must be submitted to a jury without any indication of the authorship of each proposal. The members of the jury must be independent of the participants, and when the participants are required to possess a particular professional qualification so also must at least one third of the jury.

No later than 48 days after the jury has made its selection an award notice must be sent to the *Official Journal* in the form set out in Part G of Schedule 2.

Subsidised contracts

Sometimes a contracting authority must impose, upon a body that it is subsidising, a condition that it comply with the Regulations (see regulation 25). The obligation arises when the following conditions apply:

- The contracting authority undertakes to contribute more than half the consideration for a contract.

- The contract would be a public services contract if the subsidised body were a contracting authority.

- The contract is entered into by a person (the 'subsidised body') other than a contracting authority.

- The contract is for the carrying out of services in connection with the carrying out of any of the activities in Group 502 of the General Classification of Economic Activities in the EC (construction of roads bridges railways etc.) or for the carrying out of building work for hospitals, sports recreation and leisure facilities, school and university buildings or buildings for administrative purposes.

In such a case the authority must make it a condition that the subsidised body complies with the provisions of the Regulations in relation to the contract as if it were a contracting authority, and must ensure that the subsidised body either does so or repays the contribution. This provision is in substance the same as that in regulation 23 of the Works Regulations.

Reports

A contracting authority is obliged to send a report to the Treasury every alternate year specifying for the year preceding the year in which the report is made the consideration for each public works contract, the procedure used, if the negotiated procedure was used the grounds for so doing, the category of works under the contract, and the nationality of the person to whom it was awarded. Reports containing other information required by the Treasury for the purpose of informing the Commission may also be required (see regulation 28).

Responsibility for reports

If the authority is not a minister of the Crown or a government department, the report mentioned in the last paragraph, and the other reports in the Regulations that are required to be sent to the Treasury, must be sent to the minister most closely connected with the functions of the contracting authority, and he is responsible for passing it on to the Treasury.

Chapter 8

Utilities

Procurement in the private sector is governed by Council Directive 93/38/EEC (OJ L199 9.8.93 p84) coordinating the procurement procedures of entities operating in the water, energy, transport and telecommunications sectors. This is a consolidating and amending directive, which replaced the original directive for the utilities, namely Council Directive 90/531/EEC (OJ L297 29.10.90 p1). The original directive was implemented in the United Kingdom by the Utilities Supply and Works Contracts Regulations 1992, SI 1992/3279 (in force on 13 January 1993) as amended by the Utilities Supply and Works Contracts (Amendment) Regulations 1993, SI 1993/3227; the amendment came into force on 13 January 1994. Although Directive 93/38/EEC should have been implemented by 1 July 1994, a replacement for the 1992 Regulations was still not ready at the time of writing, and therefore it is necessary to rely on the direct effect of the Directive insofar as the procurement of services is concerned. The preamble states that the rules on services contracts should be as close as possible to the rules on works and supply contracts.

Definitions

The following are summaries of the definitions to be found in article 1(4) of the Directive.

A *supply contract* is defined in the same way as in the Supplies Directive: that is, it includes the purchase, lease, rental or hire purchase, with or without option to buy, of products, including siting and installation operations.

A *works contract* is defined in accordance with the Works Regulations, by reference to Annex XI (reproduced in Schedule 3 of the Regulations), which contains a list of building and civil engineering activities as set out in the General Industrial Classification of Economic Activities within the European Communities (NACE – the same as in the Works Directive), and means either the execution, or both the execution and design or realisation, by whatever means, of building or civil engineering activities referred to in the Annex. These contracts may, in addition, cover supplies and services necessary for their execution. (For the purposes of drafting notices in the *Official Journal* the new Common Procurement Vocabulary (CPV) is supposed to be used – see below.)

Service contracts are defined as contracts other than either of the above, but excluding those to do with purchase of land, voice telephony (and related services), arbitration and conciliation, securities or other financial instruments, employment, and research and development. In the latter case there is a saving: a research and development contract is treated as a service contract where the benefits accrue exclusively to the utility – on condition that the service provider is wholly remunerated by the utility.

Contracts that include the provision of services and supplies are treated as supply contracts if the value of the supplies is greater than the value of the services.

When dealing with a service contract, rather than tackling the above definition, it is more convenient to refer to the lists of services in Annex XVI, which are the same as in the Services Directive; these lists are taken from the United Nations Central Product Classification (CPC). The Classification of Products by Activity (CPA) is a Community nomenclature based on the CPC: see Council Regulation 3696/93/EEC, which brings the CPA into effect. The CPA was used for the purposes of drafting notices for publication in the *Official Journal* by the Commission, but this has now been replaced by the recommended new Common Procurement Vocabulary (CPV), which is explained in Chapter 2. It is the product code numbers in the CPV that are supposed to be used in notices.

The Directive operates a two-tier system for services. Only those services listed in Annex XVI A are subject to the full regime (the so-called *priority services*). Those in Annex XVI B are subject only to article 18 (technical specifications and standards) and article 24 (award notices have to be sent, but publication is optional).

A *contracting entity* is defined in a rather cumbersome way in article 2, which states that the Directive applies to those entities that are public authorities or undertakings, and exercise one of the activities referred to in paragraph 2 of the article; and to those that are not public authorities or public undertakings, which have as one of their activities any of those referred to in paragraph 2 or any combination thereof, and operate on the basis of special or exclusive rights granted by a competent authority of a Member State.

An entity is considered to enjoy special or exclusive rights, in particular, where for the purpose of constructing its networks or facilities it can take advantage of a procedure to expropriate property, or place network equipment on the highway, and so on. An entity that supplies gas, drinking water, electricity or heat to a network will itself be considered to enjoy special rights if the entity it supplies does.

The draftsmen of the Regulations have eschewed any attempt to reproduce the above definition of a contracting entity. Instead the term 'utility' has been used, and the relationship between a utility and its activities is indicated by a tabulation set out in Schedule I of the Regulations. Thus a *utility* is defined as a person specified in the first column of Schedule 1, such as a person licensed under section 6 of the Electricity Act 1989, or a person licensed under the Petroleum (Production) Act 1934: the second column contains a list of activities, such as the supply of electricity to a network or the exploitation of an area for the purpose of extracting oil or gas, corresponding to each utility and taking account of the various exceptions and qualifications set out in the Directive.

Activities

The Directive applies only to those entities that exercise the activities set out in article 2(2) of the Directive, the relevant parts of which read as follows:

Article 2(2). Relevant activities for the purposes of this Directive shall be:

(a)   the provision or operation of fixed networks intended to provide a service to the public in connection with the production, transport or distribution of:
(i)   drinking water; or
(ii)   electricity; or
(iii)   gas or heat;
or the supply of drinking water, electricity, gas or heat to such networks;

(b)   the exploitation of a geographical area for the purpose of:
(i)   exploring for or extracting oil, gas, coal or other solid fuels, or
(ii)   the provision of airport, maritime or inland port or other terminal facilities to carriers by air, sea or inland waterway;

(c)   the operation of networks providing a service to the public in the field of transport by railway, automated systems, tramway, trolley bus, bus or cable. As regards transport services, a network shall be considered to exist where the service is provided under operating conditions laid down by a competent authority of a Member State, such as conditions on the routes to be served, the capacity to be made available or the frequency of the service;

(d)   the provision or operation of public telecommunications networks or the provision of one or more public telecommunications services.

The article goes on to set out various exceptions and qualifications; in the Regulations these are set out in a list of exclusions and exemptions listed in regulations 6 and 9, which in turn refer to Schedule 1.

Exclusions

The Regulations apply when a utility seeks offers in relation to a proposed supply contract or a proposed works contract or a proposed services contract other than a contract excluded from the operation of the Regulations. The exclusions, which we will now summarise, are set out in regulations 6–9 (at the time of writing, reference also has to be made to the Directive for the exclusions to do with services contracts). First, there are exclusions common to all the Purchasing Directives:

- secret contracts; security contracts;

- defence contracts within article 223(1)(b) of the EC Treaty;

- contracts governed by international agreements.

Second, there are exclusions where the utility is not carrying out a relevant activity, where the activity takes place outside the Relevant States, or otherwise where there is thought to be sufficient competition to make regulation unnecessary:

- contracts other than for the purposes of carrying out an activity specified for that utility in column 2 of Schedule 1 of the Regulations;

- contracts and design contests for the purposes of carrying out an activity outside the Community (if it does not involve the use of a network within the Community);

- contracts for the purpose of acquiring goods or works to sell or hire to another person (unless the utility has exclusive rights or the other person cannot sell under the same conditions) or services contracts directly relating thereto;

- contracts by water utilities for purchasing water;

- contracts by Schedule 1 D to N utilities (electricity, gas, oil, coal) for purchasing energy or fuel for the production of energy;

- contracts by Schedule 1 S utilities (buses) where other persons are free to provide the same service in the same area;

- contracts awarded by telecommunications utilities for the exclusive purpose of enabling them to provide telecommunications services where other entities are free to offer the same services in the same area and under substantially the same conditions (See article 8 of the Directive. This exclusion was supposed to be implemented by regulation 7 and Schedule 2 of the Regulations, but the European Court has ruled that the mention there of specific utilities is wrong: *Regina* v. *HM Treasury* ex parte *British Telecom plc*, (C-392/93) [1996] All ER (EC) 411, which is discussed below.):

- contracts that the Commission may choose to exempt in the oil, gas coal or other solid fuel sector (see article 3 of the Directive).

Third, in the case of service contracts there are exclusions set out in article 1(4), and article 13 (awards to affiliated undertakings), of the Directive:

- contracts for the purchase of real property; nevertheless, financial service contracts are subject to the Directive;

- contracts for voice telephony, telex, radiotelephony, paging and satellite services;

- contracts for arbitration and conciliation services;

- contracts for issue, sale, purchase or transfer of securities, or other financial instruments;

- employment contracts;

- research and development contracts (other than those where the benefits accrue exclusively to the utility, for its own use, on condition that the service is wholly remunerated by the utility);

- service contracts awarded to an affiliated undertaking, or service contracts awarded by a joint venture to one of the utilities involved, or to its affiliate (provided that at least 80% of the affiliate's turnover in the previous 3 years derives from provision of such services; if there is more than one affiliate providing similar services the total turnover is taken into account).

Whether a contract is a service or supply contract, where supplies and services are mixed, is determined by the normal rule, namely that if the value of the supply is greater than the value of the services it is a supply contract: see article 1(4)(vi).

In *Regina* v. *HM Treasury* ex parte *British Telecom plc* (C-392/93), [1996] All ER (EC) 411, the European Court had cause to consider the way in which one of the above exclusions was implemented. Article 8 of the Directive states that it

> shall not apply to contracts which contracting entities exercising an activity described in Article 2(2)(d) award for purchases intended exclusively to enable them to provide one or more telecommunications services where other entities are free to offer the same services in the same geographical area and under substantially the same conditions.

The activity described in Article 2(2)(d) is 'the provision or operation of public telecommunications networks or the provision of one or more public telecommunications services'.

These provisions have been transposed into English law in the following way. Regulation 7(1) of the Utilities Regulations states that the Regulations do not apply to the seeking of offers in relation to a contract by a utility specified in Schedule 2 for the exclusive purpose of enabling it to provide one or more of the public telecommunications services specified in the part of the Schedule in which the utility is specified. Part A of the Schedule is so drafted as to exclude altogether from the effect of the Regulations all public telecommunications operators, other than British Telecom plc and Kingston Communications (Hull) plc. These two companies benefit only from the more limited exclusion in part B, in respect of services provided within the geographical area for which the provider is licensed, and for services other than basic voice telephony, basic data transmission, provision of leased circuits, and maritime services.

British Telecom successfully brought an action to annul this part of the Regulations. The European Court ruled that it was not open to a Member State to determine which telecommunications services were to be excluded from the scope of the Directive. However, the Court did not go so far as to agree with the argument of British Telecom that, because other companies were legally entitled to compete, the purchasing regime should not apply to its activities. The Court held that the criterion in article

8(1), namely that 'other entities are free to offer the same services in the same geographical area and under the same conditions', was a matter of mixed law and fact. Other contracting authorities must not only be authorised to operate in the market, but must also actually do so, and whether the criterion applied had to be decided on an individual basis.

British Telecom also claimed damages, on the grounds that the United Kingdom, because of its imperfect implementation of the Directive, had caused the company to incur expense and commercial disadvantage in complying with the purchasing regime. But it was unable to persuade the Court that the breach was sufficiently serious to warrant the payment of any compensation.

Thresholds

The regulations do not apply to the seeking of offers in relation to a proposed contract where the estimated value net of value added tax at the relevant time is less than the relevant threshold value. The relevant time for this purpose is defined by reg 9(16) as follows. If the utility selects suppliers in accordance with a qualification system established in accordance with reg 17, it is the date on which the selection commences; or, if the utility satisfies the requirement that there be a call for competition by means of a periodic indicative notice, the date the notice is sent to the *Official Journal*; or, in any other case, the date on which a contract notice would be sent to the *Official Journal* if the requirement that there be a call for competition applied and the utility decided to satisfy that requirement by sending such a notice.

At the time of writing the Commission had not published a notice setting out the value of the thresholds in national currencies, although it is obliged to do so every two years. It should have done so for the period from January 1996, but because of the confusion caused by the amendments made necessary by virtue of the WTO Government Puchasing Agreement the Commission has issued only an informal notice, and the following values are taken from that:

	Supplies	Services	Works
Energy Water and Transport sectors	£316,036 400,000 ECU	£316,036 400,000 ECU	£3,950,456 5,000,000 ECU
Telecoms sector	£474,055 600,000 ECU	£474,055 600,000 ECU	£3,950,456 5,000,000 ECU
Indicative notice	£592,568 750,000 ECU	£592,568 750,000 ECU	£3,950,456 5,000,000 ECU
Small lots	not applicable	not applicable	£790,091 1,000,000 ECU

For a comparison of the above thresholds with those in the other Directives please refer to Chapter 2. Rules for calculating the value of a contract for the purposes of these thresholds are set out in regulation 9. Reference should also be made to article 14 in the case of service contracts. All of these rules are subject to what is said in article 13 of the Directive, namely that utilities may not circumvent the Directive by splitting contracts or using special methods of calculating the value of contracts. The general rule is to take the value of the consideration that the utility expects to give under the contract, net of VAT. If goods are hired, and the hire period is indefinite or uncertain at the time the contract is entered into, the value of the consideration that the utility expects to give in respect of the first four years of the hire is taken. Where a supply or service contract contains one or more options, the estimated value is taken to be the highest possible amount that could be payable under the contract.

Account must be taken, in the case of financial services, of the premium payable; in banking and other financial services, of fees, commmissions, interest and other types of remuneration; in design contracts, of the fee or commission. When a service con-tract does not indicate the total cost, the basis of calculation is: for fixed-term contracts where the term is 48 months or less, the total value; for contracts without a fixed term or exceeding 48 months, the monthly value multiplied by 48.

Aggregation

If a utility proposes to enter into two or more contracts at the same time for goods or services of a particular type, it must take, as the value of the contract, the aggregate value of the consideration it expects to give under each of those contracts. And, to summarise some rather clumsy rules for supplies or service contracts, if it enters into a series of contracts, a contract that is renewable, or a contract for the purchase of goods or services over an indefinite period, it must either take the total consideration under all similar contracts during the last financial year (or the 12 months ending before the relevant time), or estimate the total amount it expects to spend on similar contracts for the next 12 months (or for the period of the contract if it lasts for a definite period longer than 12 months).

To prevent the aggregation rules from becoming too burdensome, the Regulations contain the proviso that where goods are purchased for the sole purposes of a discrete operational unit within the organisation of a utility, the decision to buy goods of that type has been devolved to that unit, and the decision has been taken independently of the rest of the utility, purchases by other parts of the utility do not have to be aggregated. The Directive contains no mention of discreet operational units, but the Commission accepts the necessity for this provision.

The rules on aggregation for works contracts, regulations 9(10) and 9(11), are the same as those that apply in the the public sector under the Works Directive (see page 106). In order to understand the provisions one has to distinguish between 'work' and 'works'. *Work* means the outcome of any work that is sufficient of itself to fulfil an economic function, and *works* means any of the activities specified in Schedule 3 of the Regulations, being activities contained in the General Industrial Classification of Economic Activities within the Communities. A *works contract* means a contract for carrying out a work or works, or under which a utility engages a person to procure the carrying out of a work corresponding to specific requirements. Under regulation 9(10) a utility must add together the value of the consideration that it expects to give under all the contracts for carrying out the work, in order to see whether the threshold has been crossed.

Thus the value of any works, for the purpose of the threshold, is taken to be the total value of the work.

Small works contracts exemption

If the consideration for a works contract is less than 1,000,000 ECU, aggregation does not apply (unless the utility chooses to apply it) if the aggregate value of the contract, and any others in respect of which the utility chooses not to apply the aggregation rule, is less than 20% of the consideration under all the contracts for the carrying out of the work.

Valuation of works contracts

Where a utility intends to provide any goods or services to the person awarded a works contract for the purposes of carrying out the contract, the value of the consideration is taken to include the estimated value of the goods and services: see regulation 9(12).

Where the estimated value of a works contract is less than the relevant threshold, and where goods that are not necessary for its execution are to be purchased under it, the estimated value of the contract is taken to be the value of the consideration that the utility expects to give for the goods, and the relevant thresholds must be calculated as if it were a supply contract: see regulation 9(13).

Framework agreements

Framework agreements are not mentioned in the public sector purchasing directives, although the Commission permits them. In the Utilities Directive there is an express provision for this kind of arrangement. A framework agreement is a contract or other arrangement that is not in itself a supply or a works contract but which establishes the terms (in particular the terms as to price and, where appropriate, quantity) under which the supplier will enter into supply or works contracts with a utility in the period during which the framework agreement applies. The value of a framework agreement is the aggregate of the values of the consideration that the utility expects to give under all the contracts that could be entered into under the framework agreement: see regulation 9(14). A utility that proposes to enter into such an agreement may choose to treat it as a contract to which the Regulations apply, but it may not use it to hinder, limit or distort competition. Individual contracts under a framework agreement do not need to be advertised.

Technical specifications

If a utility wishes to lay down technical specifications for the goods, works or services it is endeavouring to acquire, it must specify them in the contract documents. They must be defined by reference to any relevant *European specifications*. By 'European specification' is meant a common technical specification, a British standard implementing a European standard, or a European technical approval. A *common technical specification* means a technical specification drawn up in accordance with a procedure recognised by the Member States with a view to uniform application in all Member States, which has been published in the *Official Journal*. A British standard implementing a European standard is identified by its prefix, BS EN. European technical approvals are not yet available.

A list of the circumstances in which a utility may depart from European specifications is set out in regulation 11(4), but if it proposes to rely on any of these exceptions it must state in the contract notice (or the indicative notice) which of the circumstances in regulation 11(4) it relies on. The list includes circumstances where the the utility is obliged to define the technical specifications by reference to technical requirements that are mandatory under United Kingdom law (but only to the extent that such an obligation is compatible with Community obligations), and those where it is technically impossible to establish that there is conformity with European specifications. Standards relating to telecommunications equipment and information technology have to be considered separately, because a utility may depart from European standards if there is a conflict with

Council Directive 91/263/EEC (OJ L128 25.5.91) and Decision 87/95/EEC (OJ L36 7.2.87 p31), which apply in this area. Departure from European standards is allowed also where their use would oblige the utility to acquire work or works, or goods, or services incompatible with equipment already in use, or would entail disproportionate costs or technical difficulties, but in such cases it must have a clearly defined and recorded strategy for changing over to European specifications. Where the European specification is inappropriate for the particular purpose, or does not take account of technical developments since its adoption, or where the contract is genuinely innovative it is permitted to use other standards. There is a derogation where the relevant European specification is inappropriate or out of date, but if it relies on such a derogation the utility must inform the appropriate standardising body and request the revision of the specification.

If there is no European specification the utility must use standards that are in common use within the Community. A *standard* means a technical specification approved by a recognised standardising body for repeated and continuous application, compliance with which is in principle not compulsory. ISO, DIN or ANSI standards or similar would be examples.

If further specifications to complement the standards included in the contract documents are necessary they should, if possible, indicate performance rather than design or description characteristics, unless they would be inadequate.

Regulation 11(10) requires that contract documents shall not include technical specifications that refer to goods of a specific make or source or to a particular process, and which have the effect of favouring or eliminating particular suppliers or contractors. References to trademarks, patents, types, origin or means of production may not be incorporated into the technical specifications in the contract documents; but regulation 11(12) contains a proviso that permits the use of such references if the subject of the contract makes the use of such references indispensable, or if it cannot otherwise be described by reference to technical specifications that are sufficiently precise and intelligible to all suppliers and contractors, provided that references are accompanied by the words 'or equivalent'.

A utility must provide, to any supplier or contractor who

requests it, a copy of the technical specifications regularly referred to in its contracts, or which it intends to lay down as terms of a contract that has been indicated in a periodic indicative notice; where the specifications are based on documents that are available, a reference to those documents is sufficient: see regulation 11(13) and (14).

To summarise the effects of regulation 11, which is intended to implement article 18 of the Directive, the buyer must first consider whether there is a United Kingdom standard implementing a European standard, a common technical standard, or a European technical approval. If not, the buyer must chose another standard current in the Community, and if he must complement this with further specifications they should be performance rather than design or description characteristics. But otherwise, he must consider whether there is a mandatory United Kingdom technical requirement; if it is compatible with Community law he must use that. If there is no such mandatory requirement, he should consider whether any of the derogations in regulation 11(4) apply: that is, whether using a European standard would be technically impossible, would conflict with Council Directives 91/263 or 87/95 on telecommunications terminal equipment and information technology (the standardising body must be informed), would be incompatible with existing equipment or would entail disproportionate costs or technical difficulties (there must be a strategy to change to European standards), would be inappropriate for the particular purpose or not take into account recent technical developments, or would be inappropriate because the project is genuinely innovative. Generally, contract documents must not refer to trademarks, patents, and the like, unless the subject of the contract makes this indispensable, or the words 'or equivalent' are included.

Periodic indicative notices

Every 12 months a utility must send a notice to the *Official Journal* in repect of the contracts that it expects to award in the coming year that in aggregate, for each type of goods or services, exceeds a threshold of 750,000 ECU. For works contracts the threshold is

5,000,000 ECU. A periodic indicative notice means a notice in the form set out in Schedule 4, Part A of the Regulations, containing, for example, in the case of supply contracts the name and address of the utility, the quantity or value to be supplied for each type of goods or services under the contract, the estimated date of the commencement of the procedures leading to the award, the type of award procedure used, other information such as whether a call for competition would later be published, and the date of dispatch of the notice. For supply contracts the notice must contain information in respect of the contracts that the utility expects to award in the 12 months from the date of the notice; for works contracts it must simply indicate the contracts that the utility expects to award; and for services contracts it must indicate the intended total procurement in each of the service categories listed in Annex XVI A of the Directive (so called *priority services*).

The obligation to publish a prior indicative notice takes into account the thresholds applicable to each contract. There is no obligation to mention those contracts that fall below the relevant threshold: that is, for supply or services contracts 400,000 ECU (or 600,000 ECU in the case of a telecommunications utility), and for works contracts 5,000,000 ECU. A notice need not repeat the information in a previous notice, provided that it states that it is an additional notice: see regulation 13(4).

Procedures

As in all the other Directives, there are three procedures: open, restricted and negotiated. What distinguishes utilities contracts is that a greater degree of flexibility is allowed, and there are arrangements to cover approved lists and qualification systems. The Regulations allow utilities a free choice between the three procedures, provided that there is a prior call for competition. The requirement for there to be a call for competition will be satisfied by any of the following:

- if an indication of an intention to award the contract has been set out in a prior indicative notice (see regulation 14);

- if a notice indicating the existence of a qualification system for suppliers has been sent to the *Official Journal* (see regulation 17(12));

- if a contract notice has been sent to the *Official Journal*.

In this context a periodic indicative notice must refer specifically to the goods, services or works that are to be the subject of the contract; must state that they are to be sought using the restricted or negotiated procedure without further publication of a notice calling for competition; and must invite suppliers or contractors to express their interest in writing. The utility must send detailed information on the contract to those who express an interest, and before beginning the selection of suppliers it must invite them to confirm their wish to be selected to tender for or negotiate the contract.

If the utility relies on the publication of a notice (under regulation 17(2)) indicating that there is a qualification system, the suppliers or contractors must be selected from candidates who qualify under that system.

Awards without call for competition

A contract may be placed without a call for competition if the case falls within the list of exceptions set out in article 20(2) of the Directive, and implemented by regulation 15 of the Utilities Regulations. These kinds of contract may be summarised as follows:

- where there are no suitable tenders;

- research contracts;

- where for technical or artistic reasons connected with exclusive rights only a particular person can contract;

- cases of extreme urgency;

- replacement or additional goods involving incompatibility or disproportionate technical difficulties;

- unforeseen additional works or services;

- repetition works in the case of works contracts (subject to various conditions, as to which see below);

- purchases on commodity markets;

- call-offs under framework agreements;

- bargains – a particularly advantageous opportunity available for a short time at lower than market prices;

- supplies bought in advantageous circumstances on insolvencies, winding up and the like;

- service contracts that are part of the follow-up of a design contest and which must be awarded to the winner.

In the case of repetition works under an original works contract, a utility may not proceed without a prior call for competition unless the original contract was awarded after a call for competition, the utility gave notice that a contract for repetition of the works might be awarded without a call for competition, and, in determining the value of the contract for the purposes of the thresholds, it took account of the value of the repetition works.

Time limits

For the time limits see regulation 16. If a utility uses the open procedure it must stipulate in the notice, as the last date for the receipt of tenders, a day not less than 52 days from the date of dispatch of the notice; if a periodic indicative notice has been published, this period is reduced to not less than 36 days.

If the utility is using the restricted or negotiated procedure with a call for competition, the last date for receipt of requests to be selected to tender or negotiate for a contract must not be less than 22 days, and should usually be five weeks, from the date of dispatch of the notice. If a periodic indicative notice has been published, this period of 22 days runs from the dispatch of the invitation to tender or negotiate. The last date for receipt of tenders can be agreed between the utility and the tenderers, but it must be the same for all; it should, in default of agreement, generally be at least 3 weeks and in any event not less than 10 days from the date of dispatch of the invitation to tender. In fixing the time limits the utility must take account of the volume of documentation, or the need to inspect the site. Provided that the contract documents are requested in good time and that any fee is paid, a utility using the open procedure should generally send contract documents within 6 days of receipt of a request from a supplier or contractor. A utility using the restricted or negotiated procedure, whether with or without a call for competition, must send invitations simultaneously in writing to each supplier or contractor selected to tender for or negotiate the contract. There are requirements as to the contents of the invitation; the requirements are set out in regulation 16(8). The main requirements are that the invitation should contain the address to which any requests for further information should be sent, the final date for receipt of tenders and the address to which they should be sent, a reference to any contract notice, an indication of the information to be included in the tender, and the criteria for the award if they were not specified in the contract notice.

A utility using the open, restricted or negotiated procedure with or without a call for competition must provide not less than 6 days before the final date for the receipt of tenders such further information relating to the contract documents as may reasonably be requested by the supplier or contractor provided that the information is requested in good time and any fee is sent.

A utility cannot refuse to consider an application to tender for or to negotiate a contract if it is made by letter, telegram, telex, facsimile, telephone or any electronic means, provided that in the last five cases it is confirmed by letter dispatched before the date fixed as the last date for receipt of applications.

A table of time limits is set out in Chapter 2.

Prequalification

All (or nearly all) utilities operate a vendor qualification system to screen potential tenderers: therefore the Directive permits a flexible procedure for the prequalification of suppliers, service providers, and works contractors. Although the public sector directives contain rules about approved lists of suppliers, these have to do with suppliers meeting formal minimum requirements rather than a system of prequalification.

The requirements of the Utilities Directive in relation to qualification systems are implemented in regulation 17. The system must be based upon objective rules and criteria, using European standards when appropriate. An application may be refused only if the applicant fails to meet these requirements, and the qualification of a supplier can be cancelled only if he does not continue to meet them. The rules and criteria must be made available on request, and amendments have to be sent out as they occur. Suppliers can either qualify under the system, or be certified by some other person. They must be told whether they have succeeded in qualifying or not; if this decision will take longer than 6 months the applicant must be told, within 2 months, of the reasons justifying a longer period. In determining the rules and criteria that have to be met, and the question whether a person does qualify under the system, a utility must not discriminate. It cannot impose administrative, technical or financial conditions on some applicants but not on others, and it cannot require the application of tests, or the submission of evidence, which duplicates objective evidence already available. A utility must give reasons for refusing an application. It must keep a written record of qualified suppliers and contractors. It must notify a supplier in writing beforehand if it proposes to cancel a qualification, giving reasons justifying the proposal.

A notice on the existence of a qualification system (see the Regulations, Schedule 4 Part E) has to be sent to the *Official Journal* when the system is first established, and annually thereafter if the system is expected to last, or has lasted, more than 3 years.

The main practical effect of these provisions is that requests for information by utilities to their suppliers must be taken seriously. If a supplier does not respond to a questionnaire a utility will have no choice but to exclude that person from its record of qualified suppliers.

Selection

The selection of those who are to participate in restricted or negotiated procedures, whether with or without a call for competition, must be done on the basis of objective criteria and rules which the utility determines, and that it makes available on request.

Regulation 18(2) contains a list of criteria (taken from the Works and Supplies Directives – see article 31 of the Utilities Directive) that a utility may use for deciding whether or not to select a supplier. These criteria are the same, save for necessary modifications, as those that apply in public sector purchasing, as to which reference should be made to regulation 14 of, respectively, the Supplies Regulations, Works Regulations, or Services Regulations. The criteria may be summarised as:

- bankruptcy or insolvency;

- a criminal offence relating to the conduct of, or an act of grave misconduct in the course of, the business or profession;

- failure to fulfil obligations relating to social security contributions or other taxes;

- serious misrepresentation in supplying information needed for the application of the selection criteria;

- failure to meet minimum standards of economic and financial standing set by the utility;

- failure to meet minimum standards of technical capacity set by the utility.

The list is not intended to be exhaustive. Provided that the utility keeps in mind the need for objective criteria it can make its own rules, and the criteria may (see regulation 18(3)) be based on the need to reduce the number of suppliers or contractors selected to tender for or to negotiate the contract to a level that is justified by the characteristics of the award procedure and the resources required to complete it. But a utility has to take account of the need to ensure adequate competition in determining the number of persons selected.

Whereas in the public sector there are rules as to the evidence that may be required in order to establish whether the selection criteria are met (see regulation 15 and 16 of the Supplies Regulations) the Utilities Directive imposes practically no express requirements. However, article 32 of the Directive provides that, should contracting entities require the production of certificates drawn up by independent bodies for attesting conformity of a service provider to certain quality assurance standards, they should refer to the relevant EN 29000 European standards, and are required to accept equivalents.

A consortium is eligible to tender for or be included in the list to negotiate for contracts with a utility, and cannot be excluded merely because it does not constitute a legal entity. But if a consortium is awarded a contract it may, if to do so is justified for the satisfactory performance of the contract, require the consortium to form a legal entity.

Award criteria

Regulation 20 covers the criteria for the award of a contract. These are the same as those that apply in other sectors, namely the offer that is made at the lowest price, or, alternatively, that which is the most economically advantageous to the utility. Where a utility intends to rely upon economic advantage, it must state the criteria on which it intends to base its decision in any contract notice or in the contract documents. The pro-forma of the contract notice (see Schedule 4) states that criteria other than the lowest price should be mentioned where they do not appear in the contract documents. The possible criteria include those set out in regulation 20(2): price, delivery or completion date, running costs, cost-effectiveness, quality, aesthetic and functional characteristics, technical merit, after-sales service and technical assistance, commitments with regard to spare parts and security of supply. The utility, in awarding the contract, can take account of offers that offer variations on the requirements specified in the contact documents if the offer meets the minimum requirements of the utility; but there is a requirement that these minimum requirements, and any specific requirements for the presentation of an offer that includes variations, should be stated in the contract documents. If the utility will not take account of variations, however, it must say so in the contract documents.

It is not permissible to reject a tender on the ground that it is based on, or the technical specifications are defined by reference to, European specifications or national technical specifications recognised as complying with essential requirements of Council Directive 89/106/EEC (OJ L140 11.2.89 p12), which is a directive relating to standards and technical approvals for construction products.

Abnormally low offers may be rejected, but only if the utility has first written asking for an explanation of the offer, or the parts it considers contribute to making the offer so low, and has (if the criterion is the lowest price) examined all the offers and taken into account the explanation, or (if the criterion is economic advantage) taken the explanation into account in assessing which is the most economically advantageous offer. Case 76/81 *Transporoute et Travaux SA* v. *Minister of Public Works* [1982] ECR 417, [1982] 3 CMLR 382 shows that a low offer cannot be rejected out of hand. In considering the explanation the utility may take into account explanations that justify the offer on objective grounds.

A utility may reject an offer that is abnormally low because of the receipt of state aid, within the meaning of article 92 of the EC Treaty, but only if the utility has consulted the tenderer and the tenderer is unable to show that the aid has been notified to the Commission under Article 93 of the EC Treaty or has received the Commission's approval. Article 92 states that aid that distorts or threatens to distort competition, insofar as it affects trade between Member States, is incompatible with the common market. There is a system under Article 93 whereby the Commission keeps under review aid granted by Member States; if the Commission finds that aid is not compatible with the common market it may decide that the state concerned should abolish that aid.

A utility that rejects a tender because of the receipt of state aid must send a report to the minister for onward transmission to the Commission; this is because of the duty of the Commission, under Article 93 of the Treaty, to keep under review the aid systems in Member States.

Third-country offers

Regulation 21 implements article 36 of the Directive, and states that a utility need not accept a supply contract of third-country origin. This is known as *Community preference*, and without it third countries would be able to take advantage of the public procurement regime without any incentive to open up their own markets. In essence the rules say that a utility does not have to accept offers of third-country origin, and if all things are equal must not; all things are treated as equal if there is no more than 3% difference in price. This kind of provision does not appear in the other purchasing directives. It does not apply to the purchase of services, for the practical reason that services usually have to be provided from within Member States, and the Commission felt that no useful purpose would be served by imposing restrictions on them. However, articles 37 and 38 of the Directive provide for Member States to inform the Commission about any difficulties encountered in relation to third-country service contracts, and the Commission is to keep under review and may propose to restrict the award of such contracts. Largely, this area has been taken care of by the WTO Government Purchasing Agreement, which will apply to many third-country contracts. A third-country offer means an offer to enter a supply contract under which more than 50% of the value of the goods offered originate in countries that have not concluded agreements ensuring access to their markets. Reference should also be made to Council Regulation 802/68/EEC (OJ L148 28.6.68 p1) on the common definition of the concept of the origin of goods as now incorporated in Council Regulation 2913/92/EEC (OJ L302 19.10.92 p1).

Where an offer from such a third country is equivalent to an offer from elsewhere, the utility must not accept the third-country offer, unless that would oblige the utility to acquire goods having technical characteristics different from those of existing goods, or an installation resulting in incompatibility, technical difficulties in operation and maintenance or disproportionate costs. An offer is said to be equivalent on price if the offer that is not of third-country origin is the same as or not more than 3% greater than the other offer; if the basis of the award is the most economically advantageous, then if the price is equivalent on that test, and if the offer is at least as economically advantageous, the offer must be treated as equivalent.

The WTO Government Purchasing Agreement had limited the operation of Community preference in respect of those countries that are signatories. There is a Commission notice concerning this agreement, which states that article 36 of the Utilities Directive shall not apply in the fields listed in the notice to tenders comprising products originating in the countries listed (95/C 332/05).

Award notice

Not later than two months after the award of a supply, works or services contract to which the Regulations apply, the utility must send to the *Official Journal* a notice in the form set out in Schedule 4, containing details including the nature of the contract, nature of the goods works or services provided, form of the call for competition, award procedure, number of tenders received, date of the award, and name and address of the successful contractor. If there was no prior call for competition there is a requirement to state the particular paragraph of regulation 15(1) that was relied on, and say, if it was a bargain purchase under regulation 15(1)(j), what price was paid.

Records

Part VI of the Regulations imposes certain requirements to keep records. Under regulation 25, which implements article 41 of the Directive, a utility must keep records in connection with the following:

- qualification and selection of suppliers, service providers and contractors;
- the award of contracts;
- the use of non-European specifications;
- the use of procedures that do not require a call for competition;
- the non-application of titles II, III and IV of the Directive in accordance with derogations in title I.

In the latter case the utility (when it decides not to apply the Regulations, because the contract is below the threshold or within one of the various exclusions) must keep sufficient records to be able to justify the decision. Records have to be kept for at least 4 years from the award of the contract. In addition to the above, there is a requirement under regulation 17 to keep a written record of qualified suppliers under any prequalification system. And the utility must retain evidence of the date of dispatch of notices sent to the *Official Journal*.

Under regulation 26, annual statistical reports must be sent to the minister responsible for the utility, for onward transmission to the Commission, specifying the aggregate value, estimated if necessary, of the consideration payable under the contracts awarded in the previous year that would, if they were not below the threshold, be covered by the Regulations. A minister may, from time to time, require a utility to provide a report containing such information as he may require in respect of a particular contract. The minister can require a utility to specify the activities that it considers do not fall within the purview of the Regulations, because they are not specified in Schedule 1 or are outside the territory of the Communities. And the minister can require the utility to specify the goods and works that it considers that it buys in order to sell or hire and which, in the absence of an exclusive right, are not subject to the purchasing procedures. In the latter case the utility can indicate that the information is of a sensitive commercial nature and request that it be not published.

Employment protection

Regulation 23 concerns obligations relating to employment protection and working conditions. Article 29 of the Directive states that a contracting entity may state in contract documents, or be obliged by a Member State so to do, the authority or authorities from which a tenderer may obtain information on obligations relating to employment protection or working conditions in a Member State where works or services are to be executed. Regulation 23 lays down no obligation in that regard, but does state that if a utility includes such information in the contract documents it must request contractors, or (presumably) service providers, to indicate that they have taken account of those obligations in preparing their tender or in negotiating the contract.

Subcontracting

Under regulation 24 a utility may require a tenderer to indicate in his tender which part of the contract if any he intends to sub-contract.

Confidentiality

A utility that makes information available to a supplier or contractor pursuant to these Regulations may impose requirements on him for the purpose of protecting the confidentiality of information.

Chapter 9

Remedies

Two directives make arrangements for the enforcement of obligations under the Supplies, Works, Services and Utilities Directives. These are the so-called *Compliance Directive*, Council Directive 89/665/EEC of 21 December 1989 on the coordination of the laws, regulations and administrative provisions relating to the application of review procedures to the award of public supply and public works contracts (OJ L395 30.12.89 p33); and the *Remedies Directive*, Council Directive 92/13/EEC of 25 February 1992 coordinating the laws, regulations and administrative provisions relating to the application of Community rules on the procurement procedures of entities operating in the water, energy, transport and telecommunications sectors (OJ L76 23.3.92 p14). These two directives are implemented by Part VII of each of the Supplies, Works, Services, and Utilities Regulations, which provide a statutory remedy whereby an aggrieved contractor, supplier or service provider may obtain damages and other relief by means of an action in the High Court.

The scope of the duty of Member States to implement the Remedies Directive is summarised in article 1(1) of the Directive, as amended by article 41 of the Services Directive:

> The Member States shall take the measures necessary to ensure that, as regards contract award procedures falling within the scope of the Works, Supplies and Services Directives decisions taken by contracting authorities may be reviewed effectively and ... as rapidly as possible ... on the grounds that such decisions have infringed Community law in

the field of public procurement or national rules implementing that law.

The reasons for, and extent of, the remedies for breaches of the purchasing regulations may be understood by reference to the preamble of the Utilities Remedies Directive 92/13/EEC. This states that the existing arrangements were not adequate, that guarantees of transparency and non-discrimination are necessary, that effective remedies must be available, that claims for damages must always be possible, and that in order to claim the costs of participating in an award a plaintiff should not be required to prove that the award would have been made to him. The preamble acknowledges that a supplier may not necessarily seek a review, and therefore the Commission should be able to bring the infringement to the notice of the Member State so that appropriate action can be taken. Finally it is noted that there should be arrangements for conciliation. In this chapter we shall consider the statutory remedy provided by the Purchasing Regulations, the alternative of an action for breach of contract, the possibility of judicial review or an action for breach of statutory duty, and the avenues of complaint by way of the Commission. We shall also look at procedures for conciliation and attestation.

The statutory remedy

The Regulations provide a statutory remedy whereby an aggrieved supplier may obtain damages and other relief by means of an action in the High Court. Taking the Supplies Regulations as our example, we find that the obligation to comply with the Regulations is a duty owed to suppliers, and from regulation 4 we find that a supplier means a person who sought, or who seeks, or who would have wished to be the person to whom a public supply contract is awarded and who is a national of a Relevant State. This remedy is sufficient for most purposes, but there are common law alternatives. It is likely, for example, that the supplier will wish to bring a plain action for breach of contract in combination with the statutory remedy; we shall consider this possibility below.

The Utilities Regulations are more extensive than the other Regulations in two respects: they contain provisions for a supplier who would have had a real chance of being awarded a contract to claim damages for costs of preparing the tender and participating in the procedure leading to the award of the contract (regulations 30(7) and (8)); and they contain a procedure for conciliation (regulation 31), which we shall consider below – see page 192. The mention of damages arising out of the loss of a real chance of being awarded a contract would appear to be declaratory, because all the Regulations state that damages are available to the supplier who suffers 'in consequence' of any breach; it follows that although the other regulations contain no mention of the costs of preparing the tender as part of the heads of damages they would nevertheless comprise a legitimate part of the claim.

The United Kingdom was free to devise its own method for implementing the Directives. It chose to create a High Court action that adopts some characteristics of judicial review. For convenience we shall refer to Part VII of the Supplies Regulations, where the procedure is set out in terms identical to those found in the other regulations (save for the provisions concerning the conciliation procedure, which appear only in the Utilities Regulations). Under regulation 29(1) of the Supplies Regulations the obligation of a contracting authority to comply with the relevant parts of the Regulations, and any enforceable Community obligation, is a duty owed to the supplier. The breach of a duty is not a criminal offence but any breach is actionable by a supplier who in consequence suffers, or risks suffering, loss or damage.

The action may be begun only in the High Court. Proceedings may not be brought until the plaintiff has first informed the contracting authority of the breach or apprehended breach of the duty, and of his intention to bring proceedings under the Regulations. Proceedings may be brought only if they are brought promptly and in any event within 3 months from the date when grounds first arose, unless the Court considers that there is good reason for extending that period.

There is nothing in the Directives to suggest that there should be any special time limit for bringing proceedings, and, bearing in mind that in an analogous claim in contract the limitation period would be 6 years, it is questionable whether this limitation is lawful. We shall take an analogy from another area of the law. In *Emmott* v. *Minister for Social Welfare and AG* (C-208/90) [1990] ECR I-4269, [1991] 3 CMLR 894, [1991] IRLR 387 ECJ, Mrs Emmott claimed that she should be have been paid disability benefit at the same rate as men. The Irish Government asserted that her action for judicial review was out of time. Under Irish law her action had to be brought within 3 months of the event. The European Court held, however, that in the absence of Community rules on the subject it was for the domestic legal system of each Member State to determine the procedural conditions governing actions at law intended to ensure the protection of rights that individuals derive from the direct effect of Community law, provided that such conditions are not less favourable than those relating to similar actions of a domestic nature nor framed so as to render virtually impossible the exercise of rights conferred by Community law. It is submitted that there is no reason why similar reasoning should not apply to the time limits set for proceedings brought under the Purchasing Regulations.

If the limitation in the Regulations is lawful, the effect would appear to be analogous to the position with regard to judicial review. The requirement that in any event the action should be begun promptly mirrors the rule in the Divisional Court, RSC Order 53 rule 4. In *R* v *Stratford on Avon Council* ex parte *Jackson* [1985] 1 WLR 1319, [1985] 3 All ER 769, it was held that the fact that an application for judicial review was made within the 3 months period did not necessarily mean that it had been made promptly. A good example of the operation of this rule in practice is *R* v. *Independent Television Commission* ex parte *TV NI Ltd, The Times*, 30 December 1991. On 16 October 1991 the Independent Television Commission announced the list of lucky companies to whom it proposed to grant regional Channel 3 licences. TV NI Ltd was sad to see that it was not on the list. Another disappointed company, TSW, asked for leave to apply for judicial review, but was turned down by Mr Justice Simon Brown. In the light of that refusal TV NI decided that there was no point in its applying for leave. On 4 December the Television Commission granted licences to the companies on its list (save only for West Country Television, who were the rivals of TSW).

Then, as luck would have it, TSW was granted leave by the Court of Appeal. TV NI Ltd now decided to apply for judicial review; its application was well within the 3 months time limit, but nevertheless it was refused leave, because, said the Court of Appeal, it had not acted promptly enough and once the licenses were granted a new situation arose where the Court was reluctant to interfere because third parties were affected.

The requirement to send a letter before action is intended to implement article 1(3) of the Compliance Directive, the object being to avail the contracting authority of an opportunity to put right the grievance; it was quite unnecessary to make common sense into a rule of law, and there will be silly disputes over whether the letter was written or contained the right words.

As to whether the court should extend the period during which proceedings may be brought, if the practice in judicial review proceedings is to be the guide, the test will be whether there is a reasonable excuse for the delay and good reasons for extending time. An interesting question is whether the court may still consider that undue delay would be a bar to relief when it has extended the time for bringing the proceedings. In the judicial review case of *R* v. *Dairy Produce Quota Tribunal* ex parte *Caswell* [1989] 1 WLR 1089, [1989] 3 All ER 205 (affirmed [1990] 2 AC 738), it was said that although the judge had granted an extension of time in which to bring proceedings it was still open to the Divisional Court to refuse relief, because of the undue delay, and on the ground of detriment to good administration. It was, however, the wording of the Supreme Court Act 1981 that drove the court to that conclusion.

If it is necessary to extend the period 'within which proceedings may be brought' there is a problem whether it would be too late to do so after proceedings are commenced: do you have to apply for leave first? In judicial review proceedings there is a preliminary stage at which leave has to be asked for, but there is no provision for this in the Regulations. In the Limitation Act 1980 the analogous provision is section 33, which permits the court 'to allow an action to proceed' where the limitation period has expired; in circumstances where that Act applies it is not necessary first to obtain the leave of the court. Because of the difference in wording from the Limitation Act, and because the proceedings are analogous to judicial review, it appears that in proceedings under the Public Purchasing Directives the intention is that the application to extend time for bringing proceedings must take place before the writ is issued.

Damages are available to the supplier in an action against a contracting authority, but there is a problem in quantifying his loss, because, if he cannot show that he would have been awarded the contract, he cannot show any visible loss. Regulation 30(7) of the Utilities Regulations, which is designed to implement article 1(7) of the Utilities Remedies Directive, says that where the court is satisfied that a supplier, contractor or service provider would have had a real chance of being awarded a contract, if that chance had not been adversely affected by a breach of the duty owed to him by the utility, he shall be entitled to damages amounting to his costs in preparing his tender and in participating in the procedure leading to the award of the contract. That, however, does not affect a claim that he has suffered other loss or damage or that he is entitled to relief other than damages. If he has lost the chance to participate in a valuable contract that chance does have a value. There is, moreover, a principle of Community law that sanctions must be both effective and proportionate. See for example the comments of Advocate General Van Gerven in Case C-271/91 *Marshall* v. *Southampton Area Health Authority (No 2)* [1993] 4 All ER 586 at 604:

> Community law should be penalised not only in a sufficiently enforceable manner but also in a comparable manner, that is to say under procedural and substantive conditions which are analogous to those applicable to corresponding infringements of national law.

The English law on the valuation of a chance is illustrated by *Chaplin* v. *Hicks* [1911] 2 KB 786. What happened was that in 1908 Mr Hicks, a theatrical agent, weary of more conventional methods of recruitment, placed an advertisement inviting young ladies to send him their photographs, upon the promise that the readers of a newspaper would select a shortlist of the 50 prettiest, from whom he would chose 12 to whom he would offer engagements upon the stage at £5 per week. The lovely Miss Chaplin won the readers' hearts and was placed first on the shortlist. Mr Hicks invited her to an interview, but unfortunately Miss Chaplin was in Dundee and did not receive his letter in time. The other ladies attended and 12 were selected. Miss Chaplin sued, claiming that Mr Hicks had not taken reasonable measures to tell her about the appointment; the jury awarded her a substantial sum. Mr Hicks appealed arguing that all she had lost was a chance, and that was a thing of no value. Lord Justice Vaughan Williams (the father of the composer) said that many were the cases in which it was difficult to apply definite rules; nevertheless the jury were entitled to view the plaintiff as having been deprived of a thing that had a money value.

Damages will be discounted proportionately to take account of the likelihood or otherwise of the plaintiff's deriving a benefit from his chance, as was done in *Kitchen* v. *Royal Air Force Association* [1958] 1 WLR 563, [1985] 2 All ER 241, where a solicitor had allowed a claim to become statute barred and the damages were discounted by one third because the action might not have succeeded in any event. But all this is subject to a rule of reason: no damages will be awarded if the chance is no more than a speculative possibility – see *Obagi* v. *Stanborough (Developments) Ltd The Times* 15 December 1993, [1993] EGCS 205, and *Davies* v. *Taylor* [1974] AC 207, [1972] 3 WLR 801, [1972] 3 All ER 836.

Interim relief

Interim relief is available. Under regulation 29(5) the court may suspend the procedure leading to the award of the contract, or may suspend the implementation of any decision or action taken by the contracting authority in the course of the procedure. If it decides that a decision or action taken by the authority was a breach of its duty, the court may set aside the decision or action or amend any document, or award damages, or do both; injunctions may be granted against the Crown because sections 21 and 24 of the Crown Proceedings Act 1947 do not apply.

In proceedings under the regulation the court has no power to order any remedy (other than an award of damages in respect of a breach of duty) if the contract in relation to which the breach occurred has been entered into. A problem that arises here is what is to happen if no contract is entered into – where the contract is awarded in house. The answer is most probably that the contracting authority cannot be ordered to set aside its decision, because the Regulations must be interpreted purposively.

Breach of contract

There is no reason why a breach of contract (for which the limitation period is 6 years) may not, in an appropriate case, be pleaded in combination with an allegation of breach of a duty under the Regulations. But it is important to realise there will be only a 3-month time limit for the claim under the Regulations, and there must be letter before action, which must mention the intention to bring proceedings under the Regulations.

As to the circumstances in which a contractual claim may arise, the following is an illustrative case. Visitors to Blackpool have these many years past enjoyed pleasure flights from Blackpool Airport, along the sands and over the pier. *Blackpool and Fylde Aero Club Ltd* v. *Blackpool Borough Council* [1990] 1 WLR 1195, [1990] 3 All ER 25 concerns a dispute about an invitation to tender for the right to operate these pleasure flights. The Aero Club had a concession that was due to expire in 1983, and shortly before the expiry date the council, which owned the airport and raised revenue by granting the concession, prepared an invitation to tender which it sent to the club and six other parties. The invitation said that the council did not bind themselves to accept any tender, and that no tender received after the last date and time specified would be accepted. Mr Bateson, for the club, carefully filled in the tender form, put it in an envelope, and, not trusting the post, went to the town hall himself, where he put the bid in the letterbox. Unfortunately the town hall staff did not empty the letterbox until after the deadline, and the tender from a rival, Red Rose Helicopters, was accepted. Mr Bateson complained, and the council, having established that the tender had been delivered in time, found itself in a quandary. First of all it decided to go through the formalities a second time, and further tenders were submitted, but Red Rose Helicopters then complained that they had already been granted the contract. The council therefore decided to disregard the tenders it had received the second time, and to honour the contract with Red Rose Helicopters.

In the Court of Appeal the council said that the invitation to tender was no more than a proclamation of willingness to receive offers. Lord Justice Bingham rejected that argument, holding that a contract was to be implied because the tenders were solicited from selected parties all of them known to the council, the invitation prescribed a clear, orderly and familiar procedure, and therefore the tenderer was protected at least to the extent that if he submitted a conforming tender before the deadline he was entitled to have his tender considered, or at least considered if others were.

The lesson to be learned from this case, although it did not, as it happens, involve the Purchasing Directives, is that an invitation to tender may bind the purchaser in contract to consider all the offers that are made. This principle would apply to offers received under a restricted procedure, but perhaps not to those received under an open procedure.

Judicial review

Judicial review is a remedy against persons or bodies who perform public law functions. A utility, though not necessarily itself a public body is, it is submitted, when exercising its duties under the Utilities Regulations, performing a public law function. The European Court would categorise a utility to be an emanation of the State: see *Foster* v. *British Gas plc* (C-188/89) [1990] ECR I-3313, [1990] 2 CMLR 833.

The main obstacle to the use of the judicial review procedure in cases involving public purchasing is that, save in the most exceptional circumstances, it will not be exercised where other remedies are available and have not been used: see *R* v. *Epping and Harlow General Commissioners* ex parte *Goldstraw* [1983] 3 All ER 257. Exceptional circumstances would be such as those in *R* v. *Chief Constable of Merseyside Police* ex parte *Calveley* [1986] QB 424, [1986] 2 WLR 144, [1986] 1 All ER 257, when the Court of Appeal considered that a delay in bringing disciplinary charges against some police officers was such a serious breach of the Police Regulations that judicial review would be granted without requiring the applicants to exercise their right of appeal to the Secretary of State.

However, the statutory remedy under the Regulations is open only to someone who sought, who seeks, or who would have wished to be awarded, a contract and who is a national of a Relevant State. Ratepayers, foreigners from outside the Relevant States, subcontractors, and others indirectly affected by the operation of purchasing procedures may still have resort to judicial review. The main difficulty for them will be *locus standi*, as to which a useful object lesson is *Inland Revenue Commissioners* v. *National Federation of Self Employed and Small Businesses* [1982] AC 617, [1981] 2 WLR 72) [1981] 2 WLR 722. An applicant for judicial review must first show that he has a sufficient interest in the matter to which his application relates (see RSC O.53 r.3(7)). The National Federation for the Self Employed tried to bring proceedings to impeach a decision of the Inland Revenue whereby the latter had granted an amnesty to some casual print workers in respect of their tax affairs. Lord Wilberforce said that as a matter of general principle a taxpayer had no sufficient interest in asking the court to investigate the tax affairs of another tax payer or to complain that the latter had been over- or under-assessed. This case might be applied by analogy were a ratepayer, for example, to endeavour to claim that he had *locus standi* to challenge the purchasing procedures of his local authority.

One other circumstance in which judicial review may become relevant is where a purchasing authority uses the public purchasing procedures, or analogous procedures, in a case where the purchase is below the relevant threshold, or where the Regulations are excluded. In such a case, though the Regulations would not apply, the procedure might still be challenged by reason of its unfairness, or because of a breach of Article 30 of the Treaty, as was the case in C-45/87 *Commission* v. *Ireland* [1988] ECR 4929, [1989] 1 CMLR 225. The only procedure, apart from an action for breach of contract, by which a purchasing procedure falling outside the Purchasing Directives might be challenged would appear to be judicial review.

The conclusion one arrives at is that because of its discretionary and public law nature, judicial review is not likely to feature in the development of the law of public purchasing. But there are analogies to be made between the statutory remedy and judicial review (the time limits, for example, are the same), and therefore its main features are summarised in the following two paragraphs.

Judicial review is supervisory not appellate. It covers a range of remedies: certiorari, mandamus, prohibition, declaration, damages, and injunction. Certiorari is an order quashing the decision of a public body. Mandamus is an order requiring it to carry out its duty. Prohibition restrains a public body from acting outside its jurisdiction. It is necessary to obtain leave before making the substantive application. It is discretionary and the applicant must show sufficient interest, that is to say *locus standi*. There is a 3-month time limit (see RSC O.53 r.4) for bringing proceedings.

The possible grounds for judicial review are summarised by Lord Diplock in *Council of Civil Service Unions* v. *Minister for Civil Service* [1985] AC 374, [1984] 1 WLR 1174, [1984] 3 All ER 935 as, firstly illegality, secondly irrationality, and thirdly procedural impropriety. The procedure is very simple. The application for leave is made *ex parte* on Form 86A, which is available, together with notes for guidance, from the Crown Office. There is no oral hearing at this stage unless the applicant expressly asks for one; the papers are simply considered by the judge. If the judge refuses leave the application can be renewed in open court. If leave is granted, the applicant must serve notice of motion within 14 days on the respondent and any other persons directly affected.

Breach of statutory duty

The tort of breach of statutory duty may arise in the context of public purchasing, and it is worth considering the position. In *Garden Cottage Foods* v. *Milk Marketing Board* [1984] 1 AC 130, [1983] 3 WLR 143, [1983] 2 All ER 770, Lord Diplock characterised the breach of a duty imposed by directly applicable Community law, in this case a breach of article 85 of the Treaty, as a tort of breach of statutory duty. Whether an individual can bring a common law action in respect of breach of a duty imposed by a statute depends on whether the intention of the statute, considered as a whole, and in the circumstances in which it was made, and to which it relates, imposes a duty towards an aggrieved individual: see Ex parte *Island Records* [1978] 1 Ch 123, [1978] 3 WLR 23, [1978] 3 All ER 824. There is a general rule, however, that where a statute provides a particular means of enforcement it cannot be enforced in any other manner: see for example *Stuckey* v. *Hooke* [1906] 2 KB 20. Suppliers who come clearly within the regulations will not be able to plead breach of statutory duty, and will not need to do so.

Since the decision of the European Court in Case C-6/90, C-9/90 *Francovich* v. *Republic of Italy* [1991] ECR I-5357, [1993] 2 CMLR 66, however, there is the possibility of suing the State for failure to implement a European directive, and this can be characterised as a species of breach of statutory duty, the United Kingdom having hoisted itself on this petard since the European Communities Act of 1972. British Telecom plc claimed damages in C-392/93 *Regina* v. *HM Treasury* ex parte *British Telecom plc*, [1996] All ER (EC) 411, on the grounds that the United Kingdom, because of its imperfect implementation of the Utilities Directive, had caused the company to incur expense and commercial disadvantage in complying with the purchasing regime. But it was unable to persuade the court that the breach was sufficiently serious to warrant the payment of any compensation.

Complaint to the Commission

The Commission maintains overall supervision, and imposes sanctions for disobedience to the Purchasing Directives, a system sometimes referred to as the *corrective mechanism*. There are various reporting requirements in the Regulations by which means the Commission gathers information for this purpose. The preamble to the Utilities Remedies Directive summarises the policy: when the Commission considers that a clear and manifest infringement has been committed during a contract award procedure, it should be able to bring the default to the attention of the competent authorities of the Member State so that appropriate steps can be taken for the rapid correction of any infringement. No formalities are stipulated for the form of complaint: a letter will do, but a file of evidence of sufficient clarity for the Commission to act upon should accompany the complaint.

The detail of this procedure is set out (in practically identical terms) in article 3 of 89/665/EEC and article 8 of 92/13/EEC. The Commission may invoke the procedure when, prior to a contract being concluded, it considers that a clear and manifest infringement of Community provisions in the field of public procurement has been committed during a contract award procedure falling within the scope of the Directives. The Commission must notify the Member State and the contracting authority concerned of the reasons that have led it to conclude that a clear and manifest infringement has been committed, and request its correction.

Within 21 days of the receipt of the notification the Member State must communicate to the Commission its confirmation that the infringement has been corrected; or its reasoned submission as to why no correction has been made; or a notice to the effect that the contract award procedure has been suspended, whether by the contracting authority on its own initiative or by way of an interlocutory procedure (in the United Kingdom this would be an interim order made by the High Court).

A reasoned submission may rely among other matters on the fact that the alleged infringement is already the subject of judicial review proceedings. In such a case, the Member State must inform the Commission of the result of the review as soon as it becomes known.

Where notice has been given that a contract award procedure has been suspended, the Member State must notify the Commission when the suspension is lifted or another contract procedure relating in whole or in part to the same subject matter has begun. The notification must confirm that the alleged infringement has been corrected, or include a reasoned submission as to why no correction has been made.

The next step, supposing that the answer given by the Member State was unsatisfactory, or supposing there was no answer, is for the Commission to invoke the procedure in article 169 of the Treaty. This article says that where the Commission considers that a Member State has failed to fulfil an obligation under the Treaty it shall 'deliver a reasoned opinion' on the matter after giving the State concerned the opportunity to submit further observations. If the State concerned does not comply with the opinion within the period laid down by the Commission, the latter may bring the matter before the Court of Justice. In fact, article 169 is a procedure that stands alone, and can be invoked quite apart from the corrective mechanism of the Purchasing Directives. The Commission provides a form (see OJ C26 1.2.89 p6) upon which a complaint can be made, but it is not obligatory to use this.

The Wollonia Buses case, *Commission* v. *Kingdom of Belgium* (C87/94-R) [1994] ECR I-1395, demonstrates the inadequacy of the Commission in its role of policeman. What happened in this case was that Société Régionale Walonne du Transport (Walloon Regional Transport Company – SRWT), which is based in Namur, put out an invitation to tender for the supply of some 307 buses. SRWT examined the tenders and recommended that the first lot be awarded to Jonkheere and the second to Van Hool. A third company, EMI, then sent three memoranda to SRWT relating to discounts, replacement gearboxes, and fuel consumption rates. SRWT reconsidered the tenders in the light of the memoranda and awarded the second lot to EMI. This was a failure to comply with the principle of equal treatment that underlies all of the Directives, and an example of unfair post-tender negotiation. Van Hool therefore brought an action in the Belgian Conseil d'Etat for an order suspending the operation of the decision, but this was dismissed. The Commission therefore made an application to the European Court for the adoption of interim measures suspending the contract. The Court held, however, that by allowing 3 months between receiving the complaint and informing the Member State of its intention to seek suspension of the contract the Commission did not display the diligence expected of it. The Commission must act as far as possible before the contract is concluded, or at least inform the Member State unambiguously that it intends to bring proceedings.

When the Commission invokes the jurisdiction of the European Court under article 169 there are two ways in which it may put its case. It may say that the State itself is guilty by reason of failing in its supervisory duty to stop breaches of European law, irrespective of what authority has failed to comply with a directive (see C77/69 *Commission* v. *Belgium* [1970] ECR 237, [1974] 1 CMLR 203). Alternatively, or additionally, it may allege that the State is vicariously liable for breaches by whatever entity has failed to comply with the rules. But if it relies on one failing it cannot subsequently base its case on the other. For example, in C296/92 *Commission* v. *Italy* [1994] ECR I-1 the Commission brought an action for a declaration that by allowing the province of Ascoli Piceno to award a private contract for the completion of the motorway between Ascoli and Mare the Italian Republic had failed to fulfil its obligations under the Works Directive. But in its reasoned opinion the Commission had said, putting the case in a different way, that Italy was vicariously liable for the act of the provincial administration that had failed to publish a notice in the *Official Journal*. Advocate General Gulmann was surprised, and said:

> It is not quite clear to me why the Commission formulated its claim in those terms. The formulation is surprising in view of the fact that it is established under the Court's case law that a Member State may be found guilty on the basis of objective factors of infringement of the Directive irrespective of what State regional or local body has failed to comply with the rules in the Directive.

The Court held that the scope of an action brought under article 169 is delimited by the preliminary administrative procedure. The Commission's reasoned opinion and its application must be founded on the same grounds and submissions, and it followed that the court could not consider a complaint that was not formulated in its reasoned opinion. This was not a victory for common sense, but it was well founded on the precedent of *Commission* v. *Germany* (76/86) [1989] ECR 1021, [1991] I CMLR 74.

The effect of a judgment by the European Court in proceedings brought under Article 169 of the Treaty is merely declaratory. The declaration will usually be obeyed, but if a Member State fails to comply with the Court's judgment then, under Article 171 of the Treaty, the Commission may bring a case back before the Court, and the Court may impose a lump sum or penalty payment on the Member State.

Although it is likely that the Commission will be the usual instigator of direct actions against Member States, it is possible for an aggrieved Member State to bring an action against another

Member State. Under the procedure in article 170 of the Treaty a State must first bring the matter before the Commission, which must deliver a reasoned opinion after giving each State concerned the opportunity both to submit its own case, and to make observations on the other party's case.

Attestation

Directive 92/13/EEC introduced the concept of attestation; it is not a remedy, but it was hoped that it might avoid litigation. What it entails is that utilities that comply with the procurement rules may make this known through a notice published in the *Official Journal*; this requires an independent examination of the procurement practice of the entity. In the negotiations with the Commission over the terms of the Directive the United Kingdom had proposed that instead of being subjected to the detailed rules of the Directive a utility might submit itself to a procedure for attestation of its purchasing practices. This was a good idea that the Commission did not want to understand. What the Directive says is that an entity that obtains an attestation may insert in notices published in the Official Journal the statement that:

> The contracting entity has obtained an attestation in accordance with Council Directive 92/13 EEC that, on ... its contract award procedures and practices were in conformity with Community Law and the national rules implementing that law.

This is pointless, because it provides no exemption from any of the detailed bureaucracy, and consequently there is no point in obtaining the attestation.

Conciliation

The conciliation procedure appears only in the Utilities Remedies Directive. The Utilities Regulations therefore provide, in regulation 32, that a supplier or contractor who considers that a utility is in breach of its duties, and in consequence has suffered, or risks suffering, loss or damage, and who wishes to use the conciliation procedure, should send a request to the Treasury for onward transmission to the Commission. The conciliation procedure itself is not set out in the regulation; for the details one has to look at the text of the Utilities Remedies Directive. Articles 10 and 11 state that the Commission on receiving a request must first ask the utility whether it will agree to take part in the conciliation; if it declines, that is the end of the matter. If it agrees to participate, the Commission proposes a conciliator; each party to the conciliation declares whether it accepts the conciliator and designates an additional conciliator. The conciliators can appoint experts, no more than two, to assist them; the Commission or the parties to the conciliation can reject any expert. The conciliators then give the party requesting the conciliation, the utility, and any other participants in the award proceedings an opportunity to make representations. The conciliators must endeavour to reach an agreement as soon as possible and report their findings and any result to the Commission. Either of the parties may terminate the proceedings at any time. The parties must bear their own costs and each has to contribute half the costs of the procedure, excluding the costs of intervening parties (who are responsible therefore only for their own costs).

If an application to the court is being made by a person at the same time as another contractor has applied for conciliation, the conciliators must invite the person who has applied to the court to join the conciliation. If he does not indicate his willingness to do so within the time they allow, the conciliators may terminate the conciliation if they regard his participation as necessary to resolve the dispute. Any action taken in a conciliation is without prejudice to the rights of the participants, the Commission, or anyone else to bring an action in the European Court against a Member State, or for the latter to sue another State, under Articles 169 and 170 of the Treaty.

Cabbage soup

If all else fails, the following recipe for cabbage soup will be found warming on winter evenings. First take a modest potato and slice it into slithers about the thickness of a match. In a large saucepan or casserole, sweat four or five diced rashers of English bacon so that the fat runs off. Add the sliced potato and leave to soften for a few minutes, being careful not to burn it. Add a tablespoonful of flour, sufficient to take up the fat, and plenty of black pepper. Add four pints of a good brown British beef stock. Bring to the boil and then simmer until the potato is tender. Meanwhile take a cabbage, slice it into very fine shreds, parboil, immediately refresh in cold water to stop the cooking process, and drain. Add this to the stock as soon as the potato is cooked, then bring the soup back to the boil. Correct the seasoning. Take a nutmeg and grate a little of this over the soup. Serve immediately.

Appendix

Recent Developments

The green paper on procurement

On 27 November 1996, just as this book was being completed, the Commission published its green paper *Public Procurement in the European Union: Exploring the Way Forward.* The issues addressed by this communication are as follows: the objectives of the Union's public procurement policy, its impact, the need for information and training, correlation with other policies (such as those on small and medium-sized enterprises (SMEs), on Trans-European Networks (TENs), the environment and defence), and access to the procurement markets of other countries. The Green Paper is the first step towards a general review of the procurement directives, but it advocates a period of stability. The Commission has invited interested parties to contribute to the debate in writing by 31 March 1997 and in the light of the replies it will decide whether to hold a hearing in Brussels with interested parties. It is unlikely that the debate will result in any fundamental changes in the structure of the Directives.

GPA update - utilities

It will be clear to the reader of this book that in 1997 some changes will be made to the text of the Directives in order to accommodate the Government Purchasing Agreement (as to which see page 11). The Commission has now published an amended proposal for a directive amending the Utilities Directive (OJ C28 29.1.97 p4). It is likely that the amending directive will closely follow the proposal. Article 14(1) of the Directive is to be replaced in order to bring the thresholds in line with the GPA. The reader should refer to page 43 and 159 of this book where the threshold values are those extant at the end of 1996. The figures below will be introduced in 1997, though the practical effects are minimal since the GPA limits were applied in practice from the time the GPA came into effect. The main changes are that for certain entities the GPA thresholds, given in SDRs will now apply. Certain services contracts (R & D services and certain telecommunications services) do not come within the GPA, and hence will take a threshold expressed in ECUs even when such contracts are placed by entities to which the GPA applies. Those confused by the draftsmen of the Commission proposal should read the GPA. The table of thresholds at page 42 of this book will have to be modified as follows:

Proposed utilities thresholds

Supplies
in the telecommunications sector   600,000 ECU

Works
in the telecommunications sector   5,000,000 ECU

Supplies
in the water energy and transport sectors affected by
the GPA (water; electricity; urban railway, tramway,
trolleybus or bus networks; airport facilities; and,
maritime or inland port terminal facilities)   400,000 SDR

Services
in the above water energy and transport sectors,
except R&D and telecommunications services under
CPC reference 7524, 7525 and 7526   400,000 SDR

Services
in the above water energy and transport sectors,
for services other than those mentioned immediately
above   400,000 ECU

Works
in the above water energy and transport sectors   5,000,000 SDR

Supplies
in the energy and transport sectors not affected by
the GPA (transport or distribution of gas or heat;
exploration for and extraction of oil and gas;
exploration and extraction of coal and other solid
fuels; and, railway services)   400,000 ECU

Services
in the above energy and transport sectors not
affected by the GPA   400,000 ECU

Works
in the above energy and transport sectors not
affected by the GPA   5,000,000 ECU

Proposed changes to time limits

Some minor changes to the time limits are proposed. The reader will
have to review the time limits set out in chapter 8, and the table at page
54 of this book will have to be modified in the light of the changes as
follows:

Open procedure

Last date for receipt of offers

Not less than 52 days (or, if an
indicative notice containing
certain additional information is
published, a period sufficiently
long for submission of tenders, as
a rule not less than 36 days and in
any case not less than 22 days)
from the date of dispatch of the
notice. The indicative notice must
be published not less than 52 days
nor more than 12 months prior to
the dispatch of the contract notice.
(Account should be taken of the
time required for examination of
voluminous documentation or
the need to inspect the site)

Restricted or negotiated procedures
(With call for competition)

Last date for receipt of requests
to tender or negotiate

In general not less than 37 days,
and in any event not less than the
time limit for publication in the
Official Journal (that is, 12 days
from dispatch of the notice, or

exceptionally, and if requested by electronic mail, telex or fax, 5 days) plus 10 days.

Last date for receipt of tenders

To be agreed between the utility and those invited to tender. In the absence of agreement, to be fixed by the utility and shall be at least 24 days and in any case not less than 10 days from the date of the invitation to tender. (The time allowed should be sufficiently long to take account of the time required for examination of voluminous documentation or the need to inspect the site)

Table of Cases

Table of UK Statutes

Table of UK Statutory Instruments

Table of EC Directives, Regulations, Decisions, Notices etc

Table of EC Directives

Table of EC Regulations

Table of EC Decisions, Notices, etc

References to the EC Treaty (1957)

Abbreviations

AC	Appeal Cases, Law Reports
All ER	All England Law Reports
CCT	Compulsory Competitive Tendering
CEN	European Committee for Standardisation
CENELEC	European Committee for Electrotechnical Standardisation
Ch	Law Reports, Chancery Division
CMLR	Common Market Law Reports
CPA	Classification of Products by Activity
CPC	Common Procurement Classification
CPV	Common Procurement Vocabulary
DLOs	Direct Labour Organisations
DSOs	Direct Service Organisations
ECR	European Court Reports
EEIG	European Economic Interest Grouping
EGCS	Estates Gazette Case Summaries
EN	European Standard
ETS	European Telecommunications Standard
ETSI	European Telecommunications Standards Institute
GATT	General Agreement on Tarrifs and Trade
GPA	Government Purchasing Agreement
IRLR	Industrial Relations Law Reports
NACE	The statistical classification of economic activities in the EC
PFI	Private Finance Initiative
PIN	Prior Indicative Notice (or Prior Information Notice)
RSC	Rules of the Supreme Court (procedure rules of the English High Court)
R & D	Research and Development
SDRs	Special Drawing Rights

TED   Tenders Electronic Daily
WLR   Weekly Law Reports
WTO   World Trade Organisation

Bibliography

Arrowsmith, S. (1996) *The Law of Public and Utilities Procurement*. Sweet and Maxwell, London.

Brigenshaw, D. (1995) *The European Community Utilities Directive 93/38*. CIPS, Stamford, Lincolnshire.

Digings, L. and Bennett, J. (1992 and twice-yearly updates) *EC Procurement Law and Practice*. FT Law and Tax, London.

Dunmore, T. (1994) *European Union Services Directive – a Guide for the NHS*. CIPS, Stamford, Lincolnshire.

Harvey, F. (1993) *The European Community Services Directives: A Guide for Local Authorities*. CIPS, Stamford, Lincolnshire.

Harvey, F. (1993) *The European Community Supplies Directives: A Guide for Local Authorities*. CIPS, Stamford, Lincolnshire.

Trepte, P-A. (1993) *Public Procurement in the EC*. CCH Editions Ltd, Bicester, Oxon.

Weiss, F. (1993) *Public Procurement in European Community Law*. The Athlone Press, London.

The Chartered Institute of Purchasing and Supply (CIPS) maintains a full listing of public procurement titles:

CIPS Bookshop
Easton House
Easton on the Hill
Stamford
Lincolnshire PE9 3NZ

Tel: 01780 56777
Fax: 01780 51610.

Index